Performance
Sailing and Racing

All You Need to Know to Sail Faster and Smarter

STEVE COLGATE

Chairman, Offshore Sailing School

INTERNATIONAL MARINE / McGRAW-HILL
CAMDEN, MAINE • NEW YORK • CHICAGO •
SAN FRANCISCO • LISBON • LONDON • MADRID •
MEXICO CITY • MILAN • NEW DELHI • SAN JUAN •
SEOUL • SINGAPORE • SYDNEY • TORONTO

The *McGraw-Hill* Companies

Copyright © 2012 by Steve Colgate. All rights reserved. Printed in the United States of America. Except as permitted under the United States Copyright Act of 1976, no part of this publication may be reproduced or distributed in any form or by any means, or stored in a database or retrieval system, without the prior written permission of the publisher. The name "International Marine" and all associated logos are trademarks of McGraw-Hill, Inc. The publisher takes no responsibility for the use of any of the materials or methods described in this book, nor for the products thereof.

4 5 6 7 8 9 QVS/QVS 20 19 18 17 16

ISBN 978-0-07-179346-9
MHID 0-07-179346-1
eBook ISBN 0-07-179345-3

Library of Congress Cataloging-in-Publication Data is available from the Library of Congress.

International Marine/McGraw-Hill books are available at special quantity discounts to use as premiums and sales promotions or for use in corporate training programs. To contact a representative, please e-mail us at bulksales@mcgraw-hill.com.

This book is printed on acid-free paper.

Questions regarding the content of this book should be addressed to www.internationalmarine.com

Questions regarding the ordering of this book should be addressed to
The McGraw-Hill Companies
Customer Service Department
P.O. Box 547
Blacklick, OH 43004
Retail customers: 1-800-262-4729
Bookstores: 1-800-722-4726

Contents

Preface

This book is for sailors who know the basics and want to fine-tune their sailing skills. It is for those who want:

- to sail their boats faster, better, and more efficiently;
- to overcome the fear of flying a spinnaker;
- to know what to do in emergencies; and,
- to get more satisfaction from sailing than ever before

—whether they are embarking on a day sail, taking a weekend cruise, or entering their first or their fiftieth race.

To sail fast usually means to sail well. Speed means precision of technique. Precision of technique creates self-confidence and personal satisfaction.

Sails

SAILS AND SAIL SHAPE

A boat's speed depends largely on how its sails are set and trimmed. And there are an infinite variety of sail types, shapes, and materials. Today's sails are made of many materials, including Dacron, a material that stretches constantly as the forces on it change. With the invention of Kevlar and spectra—sail material that doesn't stretch—sails are now being built with a set shape, and it is not as necessary to control the stretch as before but sail shape understanding is still critical to performance sailing. Forces affecting sails include wind-strength increases or decreases, and also pressure changes on the sails when the boat slows down as it plows into waves or speeds up when it is surfing or sailing in smooth water. As you sail in these conditions you can control this stretch, and thereby the shape of the sail, using numerous adjustment devices. We'll get to those in a bit, but before we look at the specifics, let's discuss the desirable end result.

Sails power a sailboat much like an engine powers a car with a manual transmission. When a car is moving slowly, uphill, or over a bumpy terrain, you keep it in low gear to add power. As it picks up speed and the ground levels, you shift to a higher gear. When the car is moving fast on a smooth road, you shift to an even higher gear. So, too, with a sailboat. Full sails are

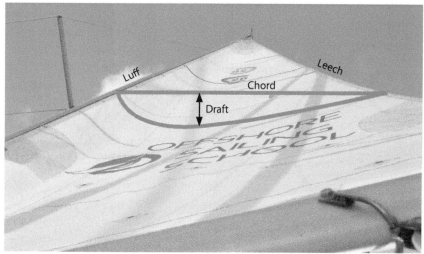

Figure 1-1. Draft is the maximum depth of the sail measured from the chord—an imaginary straight line from luff to leech. Here it's too far forward.

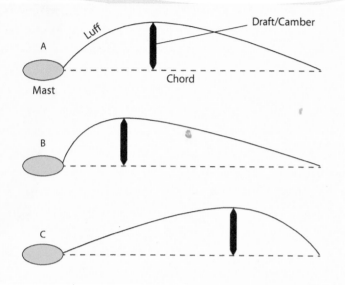

Figure 1-2. Maximum draft is shown in three positions: in the ideal position (A); forward near the mast (B); and nearer to the leech (C).

Figure 1-3. The extra material along the luff and foot of a mainsail becomes draft when on a straight mast and boom.

the low gear and flat sails are high gear. When seas are heavy and the boat is sailing slowly, almost stopping as it hits each wave, the sails need power. Full sails are the answer. In smooth water and high winds when the sailboat is moving fastest, flat sails are desirable.

DRAFT

The mainsail is a very versatile sail and can be made flat or full at will. But, you may ask, what is a "full sail" or a "flat sail"? The terms are relative. A sail is flatter or fuller than another based on the relationship of the maximum depth of the curvature (the draft) to the distance from luff to leech (the chord). Figure 1-1 shows the cross section of a mainsail. An imaginary line drawn from luff to leech is the chord. A line drawn perpendicular to the chord at the point where the sail is the greatest distance from the chord is the "draft" or "camber." The "camber-to-chord ratio" is the relation of this distance to the chord, usually expressed as a percentage. If the chord is 120" and the draft of camber is 12" deep, the camber-to-chord ratio is 10 to l or 10%. Sails can be used effectively as flat as 5% or as full as 20% at the center of effort, depending on the class of boat and the sailing conditions. The draft varies at different heights up the sail.

Of even more importance is the position of maximum draft in the sail. Figure 1-2 shows three sails all with the same camber-to-chord ratio, but with quite different locations of the maximum draft. Sail A has the draft in the desirable location for a mainsail—40% to 50% aft from the leading edge (the luff). Sail B shows the draft forward, near the mast. This can happen when a sail is designed to accept a certain amount of mast bend, but the sailor doesn't bend the mast enough as in Figure 1-1. Sail C in Figure 1-2 shows the maximum draft aft, near the leech of the mainsail. As the breeze freshens, sail material stretches and the draft tends to move aft toward the leech. This movement will cause the battens to cock to windward in the mainsail and produce a less efficient airfoil. Increased tension on the luff can keep this movement to a minimum.

The sailmaker puts draft into the sail in two ways: by a "luff and foot round" and by "broadseaming." If you laid a mainsail on the floor and "luff and foot round" was the only draft producer, it would look like the gray area in Figure 1-3. However, when it is put on a straight mast and boom, the excess material

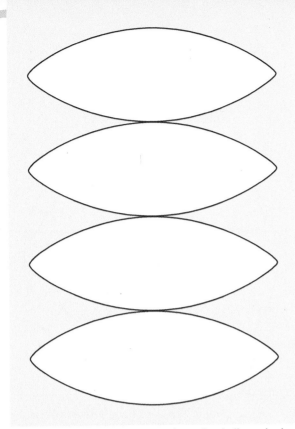

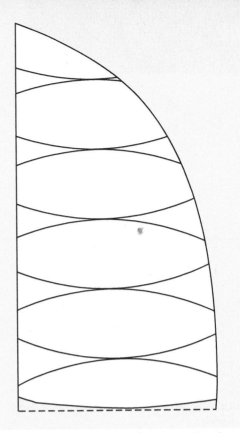

Figure 1-4. Before it's sewn together, a football may look something like this.

Figure 1-5. A sailmaker also gets draft by curving the panels and then sewing them together.

becomes draft (the white area). As the material stretches in the wind, this draft moves aft toward the desired location in the middle of the sail.

In light winds on a straight mast, the draft created by luff round will be forward, near the mast. If you bend the mast and boom to conform with the designed edge round, then the sail will be flat as a board. The other method of obtaining draft, broadseaming, is simply narrowing the panels of cloth before they are stitched together. To understand how this creates draft, imagine a football that has been taken apart. It looks somewhat like Figure 1-4. Sewn together, it becomes a football. The same method is practiced in sailmaking as in Figure 1-5. Draft created in this manner is placed exactly where the sailmaker wants it and does not depend on mast bend or stretch to place its location. A combination of both methods is used in the manufacture of all sails, except in some high-tech modern systems that use a molding process with exotic materials.

SAIL CONSTRUCTION

But first, just a bit about how a sail is constructed. The threads that run across a panel of sailcloth are called the filling threads, otherwise known as the "weft" (also called "woof") or the "fill." The threads that run lengthwise are called the "warp." Warp stretches more than weft, but the greatest stretch comes in a diagonal direction, called the "bias." Most sails are designed with this stretch in mind. For example, the mainsheet will exert the greatest force on a mainsail, and most of it will fall on the leech. Consequently, the panels of cloth are sewn together so that the crosswise threads, or filling threads, lie along the leech of the sail (see Figure 1-6).

This means that all the panels along the luff of the sail must be cut

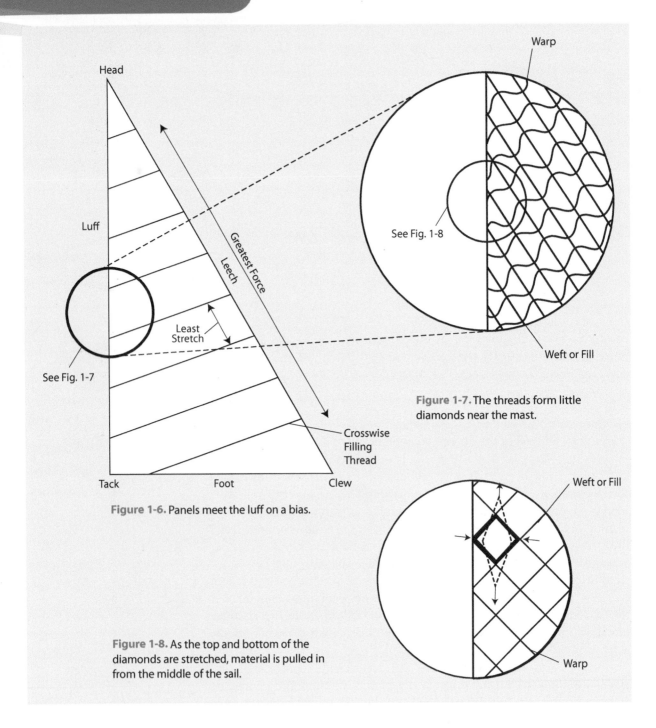

Figure 1-6. Panels meet the luff on a bias.

Figure 1-7. The threads form little diamonds near the mast.

Figure 1-8. As the top and bottom of the diamonds are stretched, material is pulled in from the middle of the sail.

on the bias, where stretch is greatest. If we were to blow up a small section of the sail along the mast, we would see that the threads look like a whole bunch of little diamonds at the bias (Figure 1-7). As we pull down on the luff and increase the tension, each diamond elongates (the dotted lines) and pulls material in from the center of the sail (see Figure 1-8). If we pull down hard on the luff when there is not enough wind to warrant it, vertical troughs or creases will appear, running parallel to the mast (Figure 1-9).

You can simulate this effect by taking a handkerchief and pulling it at two diagonally opposite corners, as in Figure 1-10. The same troughs will

Figure 1-9A. Excessive luff tension causes wrinkles near the mast.

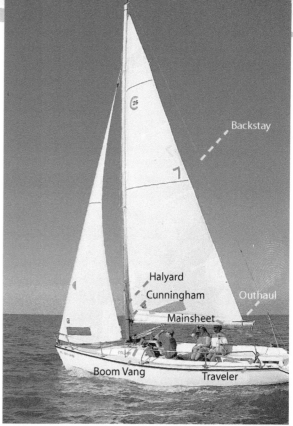

Figure 1-9B. Sail controls that adjust draft and ultimately sail shape.

appear just as they will when there is too much luff tension. Figure 1-11 shows that as the corners are stretched apart on the bias, the material moves upward. The lower corner was even with the person's waist and is now a few inches higher.

PROPER MAINSAIL ADJUSTMENT

Tensioning the Luff

There are two ways to tension a mainsail's luff—with a downhaul and with a cunningham. In the days of cotton sails, you would buy a sail that was actually too small in light air. This would allow you to stretch it with the halyard to flatten the sail when the wind velocity increased. Of course, this meant that you would automatically penalize yourself in light air by having reduced sail area.

To solve this little dilemma, Briggs Cunningham, developer of the Cunningham racing car and skipper of *Columbia*, winner of the 1958 America's Cup, chose the simple expedient of placing a grommet above the mainsail tack fitting in a full-sized sail. When the luff of the sail was stretched as far as it could legally be, a block-and-tackle arrangement was attached to a hook running through the grommet. Tightening it added further tension to the luff. Though some wrinkles do appear along the foot below the grommet when the cunningham is in use, they don't seem to make an appreciable difference in the efficiency of the sail. So just forget them.

This grommeted hole in the mainsail has become known as a "cunningham hole," and it is now commonplace in many classes of sailboats. With a cunningham, a sail can be made full-sized for light-air performance and still be tensioned along the luff to keep the draft from moving aft when the breeze increases. A variation of the cunningham is also used on jibs. Some boats have a cloth tension device attached to the jib near the tack, and a line that leads to the cockpit can be adjusted to increase or decrease the

Figure 1-10. Hold handkerchief at two corners on the bias.

Figure 1-11. Pull out and creases appear as bottom corner pulls up.

tension of the luff. The theory is the same for both a jib and a main. But the jib is much more sensitive to luff tension than is the main.

When sailing to windward, the point of maximum draft on a jib should be about 35% of the chord behind the luff, compared to about 50% of the chord in a mainsail. If the wind increases, it's far easier for the draft of a jib to work aft of its normal location, which means you must constantly change the jib luff tension for highest efficiency whenever the wind velocity changes.

Luff tension must also be changed depending upon what point of sail the boat is on. When reaching or running, you want a very full sail with the draft well aft. You should ease off the downhaul and cunningham in this situation.

The Traveler

An important mainsail adjustment is the traveler—a track with a sliding mainsheet block that runs across the boat beneath the main boom. Travelers with ball bearing cars are preferable because, when close-hauled, those without ball bearings have a tendency to stick (create more friction) under the pressure of the mainsheet. The traveler's function is to allow the angle of the boom relative to the centerline of the boat to change without allowing the boom to rise. If instead of using a traveler we ease the mainsheet, the force of the wind on the sail will lift the boom in the air and the top part of the leech will fall off to leeward.

Figure 1-12 shows the constant angle the apparent wind makes with the luff of the sail over its full length when the mainsheet is trimmed in tight. Figure 1-13 shows how this angle changes in the upper part of the sail when the mainsheet is eased.

The upper part can actually be luffing even though the bottom part is full of air. This effect is called "twist" and is undesirable, except in certain conditions.

There are a couple of exceptions. The wind on the surface of the water is slowed down by friction, so the wind at the top of the mast has a greater velocity than at deck level. Thus, the top of the sail is sailing in a continual puff relative to the bottom of the sail. Apparent wind comes aft in a puff. In order for the apparent wind to have the same angle to the luff all the way up and down, a slight twist at the head of the sail is necessary.

The other exception to the harmful effects of twist is when there is very heavy air. The upper part of the sail greatly affects a boat's heeling, just as weight at the top of the mast does. If you want to reduce heeling, simply reduce the effectiveness of the upper part of the sail by inducing twist. Instead of easing the traveler out, ease the mainsheet.

The traveler is also used to help control heeling. We all know that as a sailboat turns from close-hauled (see Figure 1-14A) to a reach, you should ease the sails. If you don't, the boat will heel way over as the wind hits the windward side of the sail at right angles to it. Forward drive will be reduced because of the lack of drive-producing airflow over the lee side of the sail (Figure 1-14B). We know that if sails are trimmed properly for a reach, the boat heels less than it does when close-hauled because the drive from

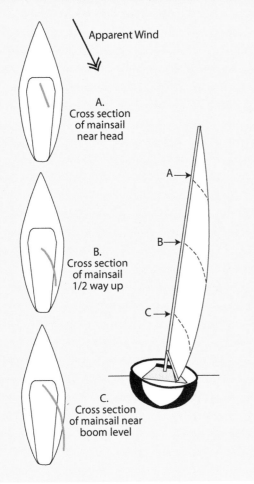

Figure 1-12. With the mainsheet trimmed tightly, the sail near the top of the mast is at the same angle to the wind as the bottom.

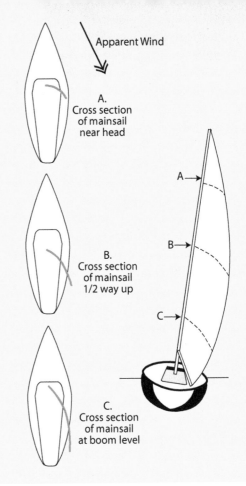

Figure 1-13. When the mainsheet is eased, the top part of the sail falls off to leeward.

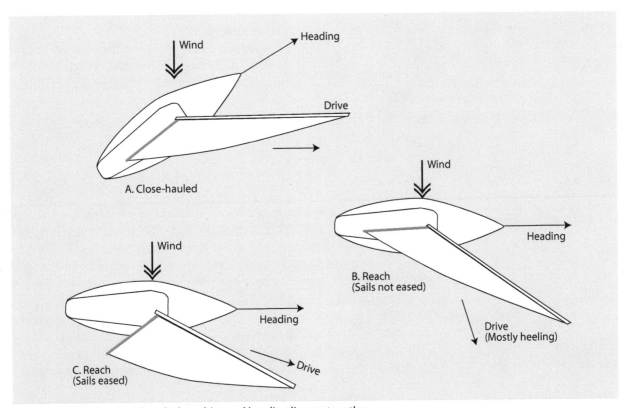

Figure 1-14. Heeling is reduced when drive and heading line up together.

the sails is more in the direction of the boat's heading, and heeling force is reduced (Figure 1-14C).

If you are heeling excessively when close-hauled, you can reduce the heeling by easing the traveler. Many good sailors use the traveler rather than the mainsheet to adjust to changes in wind velocity. Every novice has learned that when you are hit by a puff, you ease the mainsheet and head up into the wind to reduce heeling. The advanced sailor does much the same thing, but eases the traveler instead, which lowers the boom toward the leeward side, thereby reducing heel. Traveler trim depends to an extent on the type of sailboat. Since the apparent wind comes aft in a puff, easing the traveler maintains the angle the apparent wind makes with the luff of the sail.

As you fall off to a true reach, easing the traveler acts like a boom vang, keeps the boom from rising, and reduces twist. Like the traveler, the boom vang controls tension along the leech of the sail. It is most useful when sailing off the wind. When the traveler car reaches the outboard end of the track, and the mainsail must go out still farther, the traveler is no longer effective. Now the mainsheet, instead of pulling down, is angled out over the water, and a boom vang has to do the work of keeping twist out of the sail. In Figure 1-15 the vang is not in use, and the sail is badly twisted. Figure 1-16 shows the difference in the leech when the boom vang is pulled tight. The farther forward in the boat the traveler is located, the farther out the boom can go before the traveler car reaches the end of the track and the vang must take over. The closer the traveler is to the boom, the more positive is its control. If the traveler is mounted on the cockpit floor a number of feet beneath the boom, a puff may cause the mainsheet to stretch. The boom will lift and move outboard, negating some of the traveler's usefulness.

There is one other use of the traveler. You can trim the main boom up to the centerline of the boat without pulling down hard on the mainsheet.

Figure 1-15. No vang tension, mainsail twisted so top part is useless.

Figure 1-16. Vang tight, mainsail presents its full area to the wind.

Figure 1-17. **Figure 1-17.** With the traveler car to windward and the mainsheet eased, the boat on the left has a free leech (and likely better boat speed), while the boat on the right has a tight leech, resulting from a tightly trimmed mainsheet that pulls the boom down.

The closer the boom comes to the center of the boat, the higher you can theoretically point.

On a light day, however, trimming the main tight can result in a very tight leech, which impedes wind flow. The solution is to leave the mainsheet lightly trimmed and pull the traveler car up to windward, bringing the boom toward the middle of the boat without pulling it down at the same time. The boats in Figure 1-17 illustrate this point. Now let's look at the backstay.

The Backstay

The adjustable backstay is a mast bending device. On small boats, a block-and-tackle arrangement is attached to the lower end of the backstay and produces the leverage for bending the mast with a minimum of effort. Larger boats often have hydraulic backstay adjusters. Other factors are involved in mast bend such as leech tension, angle and length of the spreaders, placement of the partners where the mast goes through the deck (if any), location of the mainsheet blocks along the boom, etc. But for now let's just analyze the backstay. Tightening the backstay bends the mast and flattens the mainsail.

When the backstay is tensioned, the middle of the mast bows forward, lengthening the chord, as the dotted line in Figure 1-18 indicates, and decreasing the draft. With a longer chord distance and the same amount of sailcloth as before, the draft has to be less as the excess material that the sailmaker built into the sail along the luff is stretched out and the sail flattened. But also note the action at the top of the mast. It is pulled back and down, which effectively shortens the distance between the top of the mast and the end of the boom. The distance A to B2 is shorter than the distance A to B1. This frees the leech of the sail because the material sags off rather than being pulled tight. The end result is indicated by the shaded area in

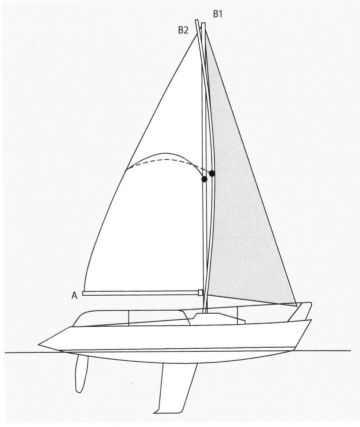

Figure 1-18. Bending the mast changes the camber-to-chord ratio and flattens the sail (see dotted line).

Chapter 1

Figure 1-19. Reduction in draft by bending mast aft.

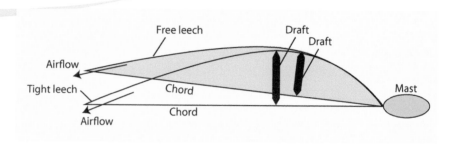

Figure 1-20. The combination of moving the mast forward and freeing the leech really flattens the sail.

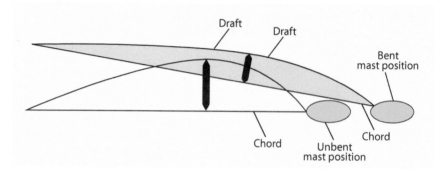

Figure 1-19. Even if the chord length remains the same, a free leech creates a flatter sail since the draft is less. Figure 1-19 also shows that the drive will be in a more forward direction, which reduces heeling. Weather helm is reduced as the leech is freed. With a tight leech, airflow on the windward side of the sail is bent around until it exits off the leech in a windward direction. The tight leech acts like a rudder, forcing the stern to leeward and creating weather helm. But when the leech is freed, the air can flow straight aft or slightly to leeward, which minimizes turning effect of the leech. Figure 1-20 shows how the combination of the mast moving forward and a freer leech creates a much flatter sail.

The Mainsheet

Mainsheet tension, particularly on light days, will harden up the leech and cock the battens to windward. The sail will look much like the unbent mast position in Figure 1-20. Figure 1-21 shows a cocked leech on the boat to the right caused by overtrimming the mainsheet. Because this is a fuller shape, we can say that mainsheet tension makes any cross section of the sail fuller, whereas an eased mainsheet, and the corresponding twist in the sail as the boom rises, makes the cross section of the sail flatter.

The Outhaul

Figure 1-21. On the right, too much mainsheet tension cups the leech (also known as a "cocked leech") of the mainsail.

The outhaul mainly affects the draft in the lower part of the sail near the boom. Figure 1-22 shows the outhaul eased, and it is obvious that it creates a greater draft in the sail. Even if the actual draft remains the same, the shortening of the chord makes the camber-to-chord ratio larger, thereby making the sail fuller. Easing the outhaul excessively will cause wrinkles along the foot of the mainsail.

HOW TO "SEE" SAIL SHAPE

It's difficult for many sailors to see fine adjustments in sail shape so it's best to use visual aids. In order to determine how much mast bend you have, with an indelible pen draw short vertical lines on the mainsail at spreader height, evenly spaced 3 inches apart. Sight up from under the gooseneck to the masthead and determine where an imaginary straight line would fall. With this method we can determine that the mast in Figure 1-23 has about 13 inches of mast bend. To see how much twist the mainsail has, sight up the sail from under the boom and line up the top batten with the boom. It should be parallel or falling off a little, but should not be cocked to weather. If there is room to stand on the afterdeck behind the main boom, you can obtain a good overall perspective of the mainsail from that position.

Colored tape can be placed on the backstay in small boats to correspond with a certain amount of mast bend. Colored marks on the mainsheet can give you a guide as to how much twist there is in the mainsail leech for given wind conditions. Marks next to the traveler at 1-inch increments can help you duplicate the traveler car position. Also, a mark on the jib halyard against a series of marks spaced at equal intervals on the mast can be helpful in duplicating luff tension.

The jib is a little harder to judge. When it is a genoa, overlapping outside the spreader, use the spreader tip as a guideline. Depending on the type of genoa, the lateral jib lead placement, the wind and sea conditions, and the luff tension, the cloth should be trimmed anywhere from a point a few inches off the spreader tips to just touching them. Many sailmakers put a "fast stripe" on genoas. This is a dark stripe midway up the genoa parallel to the deck that makes the draft in the sail very easy to see.

If the jib does not overlap the spreaders, the leech will probably point right at them. Place a piece of tape on the spreaders as a guideline and trim the sail until the leech points at the tape. One way of knowing whether the jib is trimmed in too tight or the draft is too far aft is to observe the amount of backwind in the mainsail. If the backwind extends farther back than usual, it is probably caused by overtrimming the jib.

Last, for an overall look at the jib shape, go to the bow and look at the leeward side. This can help you see if the draft has been blown aft. All the above helps you to duplicate the same shape at another time,

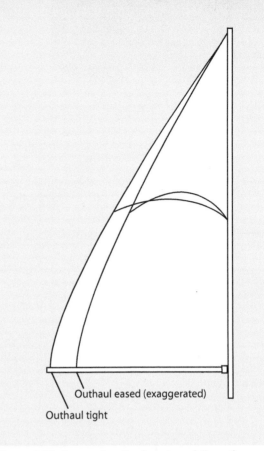

Figure 1-22. An eased outhaul creates a fuller sail.

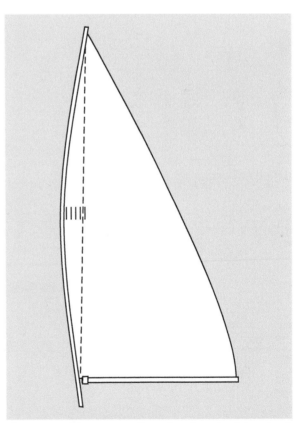

Figure 1-23. The amount of mast bend can be determined by sighting up the mast past marks placed at known intervals. In this case, the marks are 3 inches apart, so the mast bend is 13 inches.

but only testing alongside another sailboat will tell you which shape or which sail is fastest. Sailmakers do this all the time when testing sails, so it can help you too if you can find a willing collaborator with a boat equal to yours. Sail side by side close-hauled, each with clear air, keeping one boat as a "control" (don't change anything on it) and changing only one variable (such as the mainsheet tension or mast bend) on the other at any one time.

PROPER JIB ADJUSTMENT

Twist in the mainsail results from the top part of the sail falling off to leeward because of inadequate leech tension. The same problem exists with the jib. Two things determine how much twist a jib will have when beating: jibsheet tension and the fore and aft placement of the jib leads. If the lead is too far aft, the jibsheet will pull along the foot of the sail but there won't be enough downward tension on the leech. The result is that the top part of the sail will tend to luff first. Other things can have the same effect as moving the jib lead block forward or aft. For instance, if the mast is raked (leaned) aft by lengthening the jibstay (see Figure 1-24), it effectively moves the head of the sail aft and lowers the clew. If the jib lead remains in the same place, raking the mast frees the leech of the jib.

A good rule of thumb is the opening or slot between the jib leech and the body of the mainsail should remain parallel. This means if we induce twist in the mainsail in heavy weather to reduce drive in the upper part of the main, thereby reducing heeling, we must also do the same to the jib.

In light air, any fullness should be down low in the jib. You can accomplish this by easing the jib sheet. This has the same effect as easing the outhaul on the main along the boom. Easing the jib sheet increases draft by shortening the distance between the tack and the clew, and this gives you greater drive in light airs and lumpy seas. However, there is one detrimental side effect to easing the sheet. As the clew goes out, the angle of the jib sheet is lowered and frees the leech (see Figure 1-25). Therefore, to regain the proper leech tension, you must move the jib lead forward.

The jib tack, jib halyard tension, and jib downhaul, if any, also affect the location of the clew and the jib lead. You usually increase the tension on the luff of the sail to control the jib's shape as the wind increases. As the jib stretches under the force of the increased wind velocity, the draft tends to move aft in the sail, and more luff tension is required to keep the draft in the same location. But when the luff tension is increased by tightening the jib halyard, pulling the head of the sail higher, the clew is lifted higher also, and the lead will need to be placed farther aft (see Figure 1-26). In heavy air you may even want a little twist in the sail, and the lead may need to come back even farther.

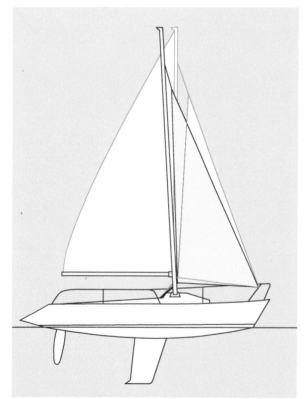

Figure 1-24. Raking the mast aft frees the leech of the jib. Move lead forward to maintain leech tension. To get more or maintain the same leech tension, you must move the jib lead forward.

Observe what jib halyard tension does to the leech of the sail. As draft is pulled forward by tensioning the halyard, the leech should become free and flatter. On high-aspect sails (those that are tall and narrow rather than wide and squat), the opposite can sometimes happen. The halyard pulls on the leech almost as much as on the luff, because the angle is about the same, so luff tension cups the leech instead of freeing it.

As a boat falls off onto a reach, the jib sheet is eased and a great deal of twist can develop. In order to correct this, the lead must go forward again. In the old days, sailboats did not have effective boom vangs for their mains and the top part of the mainsail twisted off to leeward when reaching. In order to make the jib leech match the curve of the main, sailors would move the jib lead aft.

Not so, today. Effective boom vangs keep twist in the main to a minimum and, therefore, little twist is needed in the jib. So in most cases, the lead when on a reach should go forward, not aft, to pull down on the jib leech and reduce twist.

One other sensitive adjustment for the jib lead is its correct distance outboard from the centerline of the boat. To find this point, first draw a line from the tack of the jib to the jib lead and measure the angle it makes with the centerline of the boat. This is called the "jib-lead angle," and it will vary greatly from boat to boat.

A narrow keelboat will get away with having the jib lead fairly well inboard and still maintain speed while pointing high. A beamy centerboarder, though, will have her jib leads farther outboard in order to obtain enough drive to go through the seas.

Think of the lateral placement of the jib lead in the same terms as the mainsheet traveler. If the traveler needs to be eased, the jib lead should probably be eased outboard too. The best way to tell whether your jib-lead angle is correct is to test your boat against another. Sail close-hauled alongside another boat of the same class and vary the lateral position in or out. The correct location will show up in increased speed.

You can measure the angle by using the table and diagram in Figure 1-27. To do so, first measure along the centerline from the tack fitting to any point just forward of the mast (distance AB on the diagram). From B, measure at right angles to the point that intersects a straight line running from the tack fitting

Figure 1-25. As the jib sheet is eased, the clew goes forward, the sheet angle is lowered, the effective lead goes aft, and twist develops.

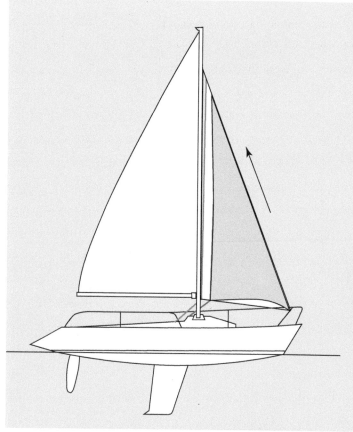

Figure 1-26. As the jib halyard is tensioned, move the lead aft.

13

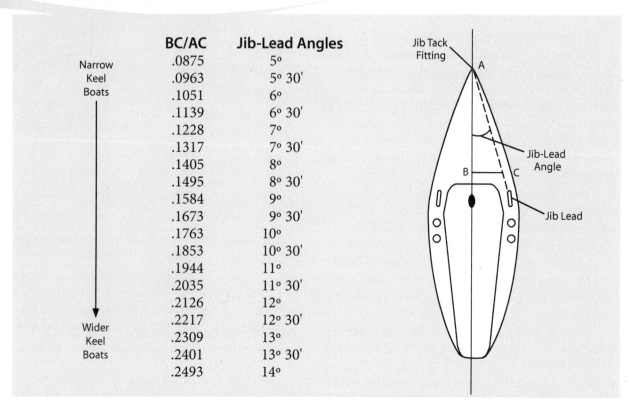

BC/AC	Jib-Lead Angles
.0875	5°
.0963	5° 30'
.1051	6°
.1139	6° 30'
.1228	7°
.1317	7° 30'
.1405	8°
.1495	8° 30'
.1584	9°
.1673	9° 30'
.1763	10°
.1853	10° 30'
.1944	11°
.2035	11° 30'
.2126	12°
.2217	12° 30'
.2309	13°
.2401	13° 30'
.2493	14°

Narrow Keel Boats → Wider Keel Boats

Figure 1-27. The smaller jib-lead angles are found on narrow keel boats. Wider angles are found on wider, often centerboard, boats.

to the jib lead (distance BC). Divide BC by AB and carry it to four places. Then consult the table for the jib-lead angle in degrees. Example: AB is 59" and BC is 11". Eleven divided by 59 is .1864, which is a hair over 10°30' in the table.

Start at about 10° on your boat and, in light air, come inboard with light jib sheet tension to about 8°. In heavy air you may be able to go outboard to 11° or even 12° with success. But remember—these adjustments always vary with boat type and the wind and sea conditions.

TEST QUESTIONS

1. What is the "draft" of a sail?
2. What is a "cunningham"?
3. What is "twist" in a sail?
4. How can you use the mainsheet and the traveler to increase twist?
5. What is "mast rake" versus "mast bend"?
6. Is a sail with a free leech fuller or flatter than one with a tight leech?
7. What controls twist in a jib?
8. Are flat sails for speed or for power?
9. What are the threads called that run lengthwise in sailcloth?

Boat Handling

HEELING

Many sailors are very uncomfortable at first when a sailboat heels. One reason is that we are used to a world that stays level, and it feels unnatural when the horizon is constantly at an angle. Heeling is of such great concern to new sailors that when I recently queried dealers on what question prospective first-time sailboat buyers ask most, the overwhelming response was, "How tippy is it?"

This fear is reinforced by news photographs of capsized sailboats, or of racing crews hiked way out in an apparent effort to keep the boat from tipping over. If the novice steps aboard a small centerboarder at a dock, he or she is further convinced that all boats are tippy, and it will take a crew having the muscles of a gorilla and the agility of a cat to sail them.

Of course, this is just not so. The first time I sailed a Finn dinghy I was scared to death that I'd capsize and make a fool of myself. Motionless in the water, dinghies are very tippy. But the minute they pick up speed they become quite stable. It is not even necessary to hike out. You can sail along quite comfortably just sitting upright on the windward side of the boat, though the boat will heel more and therefore sail more slowly.

The reason racing sailors hike out is not for survival or to keep from capsizing, but to sail the boat more upright and therefore more efficiently. The less heel a sailboat has, the more sail area is exposed to the wind and the more quickly it can go. A boat heels in the first place because the keel or centerboard in the water counteracts the tendency of the boat to be pushed sideways by the wind in the sails (making leeway). Because the keel resists leeway, the side force of the wind on the sails results in heeling. The more heeling, the more the keel is angled, and the less lateral resistance it has. In other words, greater heeling creates greater leeway.

A boat with a heavy keel can usually resist the heeling force better. However, the heavier the keel, the stronger a boat must be built, and the more it probably will weigh. A heavy boat sits deep in the water and pushes a greater volume of water aside when sailing. This increased resistance often more than offsets the increased speed obtained from the greater sail area.

Hull shape also affects heeling. As the sails fill on a tack, one side of the boat sinks into the water and the other side lifts out. When the crew sits on the high side of a wide hull, he or she obtains more leverage to resist heeling than with a narrow hull. However, another trade-off is involved. The wide hull usually has more wetted surface (square feet of area in contact with the water) and, therefore, more skin friction to slow the boat down when it isn't heeling. Moreover, it doesn't usually sail upwind quite as well, or point as high, as a narrow boat. Because of all these compromises, a wide variety of sailboat designs is available on the market. Racing sailors consider speed above all else; cruising sailors tend to look for comfort, room, and ease of handling first. But no matter whether a boat is a beamy centerboarder or a narrow keelboat, the reaction to heeling is predictable, and a skipper must make adjustments accordingly.

The one universal effect from heeling is weather helm, and small amounts of it are desirable. Weather helm (the tendency of the boat to turn toward the wind) does give the boat more feel. Instead of having to steer the boat in both directions, you only have to steer it away from the wind, because the boat always wants to turn toward the wind. With a slight constant pull of the tiller to windward, you can counteract this tendency of the boat to wander and you can therefore steer the boat in a straight line quite easily.

And with a slight amount of weather helm, the boat will automatically head up in puffs. This reduces heeling and maintains the angle the wind originally made with the sails because the apparent wind (the wind that is blowing on the sails) moves aft from the bow as the wind increases in a puff.

The close-hauled weather helm angle the rudder makes with the water is shown in Figure 2-1. We are looking down from above and imagining that the rudder can be seen through the boat. Note that the water flow over the rudder is like that of an airfoil. There is lift to windward when the rudder is at the angle in the diagram, but as you can imagine, there is an undesirable pull to leeward whenever the tiller is put to the other side of the boat's centerline. There are two reasons heeling causes weather helm. First, the curved shape of the hull on the leeward side of the bow forces the bow to windward when it's heeled. If you throw a curved piece of wood in

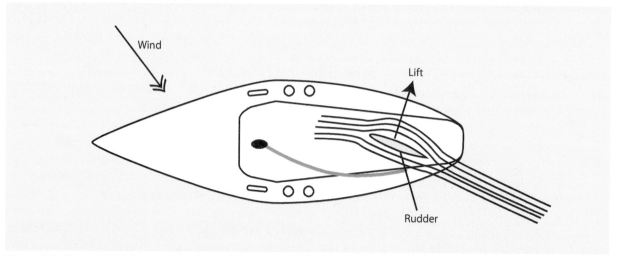

Figure 2-1. The rudder helps to reduce leeway by producing lift.

the water it doesn't travel in a straight line. Neither does the leeward side of a sailboat when most of the windward side is out of the water. Note the bow wave of the keelboat in Figure 2-2. The bow wave is much larger on the lee side, and this is forcing the bow to weather. The greater the heel, the more pronounced this becomes. Without any heeling, neither bow wave has a chance to overpower the other.

The second reason heeling causes weather helm is that it places the sail area out over the water. In Figure 2-2, if you draw a vertical straight line from the leeward edge of the hull, you can see that a large portion of sail is not over the boat. The forward pull the sail exerts is therefore out of alignment with the drag of the hull in the water, and this causes a turning moment to windward.

When heeling is excessive, weather helm becomes quite strong. Figure 2-3 shows a keelboat that is heeled way over. The rudder is being turned to counteract the resulting weather helm but is practically stalled. Also note the turbulence the rudder creates in the left of the photo. There is so much rudder drag here, the boat speed just has to be markedly slower. And, as the boat heels, the rudder comes farther out of the water and loses its effectiveness.

Excessive heeling, therefore, creates weather helm and makes sailing uncomfortable for the crew, tiring for the helmsman who is always pulling hard on the tiller, and inefficient in terms of speed.

TACKING

Now let's look at some of the basic procedures such as tacking and jibing. Most people consider these two maneuvers to be quite simple, and they are. However, good sailors refine them to an art form. I'll never forget seeing the great Danish Olympian, Paul Elvstrom, tack a number of times during a race in gusty, 20-knot winds. The smoothness of each turn was exceptional as the mast described a smooth arc from a constant angle on one tack to the identical angle on the other tack. This is what differentiates the good sailor from the beginner or experienced poor sailor.

By adjusting sail trim and steering angle, the mast stays at a constant angle to the water through gusts and lulls in the wind, and crests and troughs of the waves. The boat is not turned too far after a tack (which would cause it to heel over) nor too short causing the boat to stand upright. Also, in a proper tack the boat doesn't heel over just before a tack—a constant problem with new sailors.

Figure 2-2. Large bow wave on leeward side pushes the bow to weather (toward the wind).

Figure 2-3. Turbulence indicates a stalled rudder resulting from excessive heeling. (Courtesy Louisa Hightower)

TO CORRECT TOO MUCH WEATHER HELM

- Ease mainsheet or traveler
- Reduce heeling by hiking
- Reduce mainsail area or effectiveness by carrying a slight luff, freeing the leech, or reefing
- Put up a jib (if none up) or a larger jib
- Reduce mast rake
- Move crew or equipment aft

For some unfathomable reason, some sailors sitting on the windward side pull the tiller toward them just before they tack, causing the boat to head off and heel over. This causes a strong weather helm, so when the tiller is put to leeward and the boat allowed to tack, it spins quickly into the wind. The speed of the tack sometimes catches the jibsheet crew unaware, and the jib backs before it can be released. This forces the boat over on the other tack past 90°, causing it to heel badly. At about this point, as the helmsman is trying to steer the boat back up to a close-hauled course on the new tack, the jib finally gets released and flaps madly. With the jib no longer holding the boat down, and the mainsail and the helmsman trying to force the boat up toward the wind, the boat suddenly spins to windward. Just as the crew gets the jib trimmed in on the new side, the boat is pointing so close to the wind that the jib backs again and the whole process is repeated. On top of this, some helmsmen don't sit in a proper comfortable manner, and when the boat heels over on the new tack because of the backed jib, they slide to leeward pushing the tiller as they go. With the helm "Hard alee" they accidently tack again.

On a small boat with a tiller, the proper steps are as follows: the helmsman should make sure he or she is in a comfortable position to windward. The jib crew should take the leeward sheet out of its cam cleat so it can be readily released. The windward sheet should be wrapped two or three times around the winch and the slack taken out of it. (On a larger boat with a wheel, the same basics apply. Check to windward and aft to be sure you are not tacking right in front of another boat. Check your compass or a landmark 90° to windward to get a rough estimate of the course on the next tack so you don't turn the boat too far.)

The helmsman then allows the natural weather helm of the boat to initiate the tack. In lighter air the crew may lean in to allow the boat to heel more and accentuate the weather helm, and in very light air the helmsman may head off just slightly to increase the weather helm. Then, as the boat turns into the wind, and the jib barely starts to luff, the crew releases the jib. This helps continue the turn because the mainsail heads the boat into the wind. The helmsman by this point is steering the boat through the wind.

The reason for initially allowing the boat to turn itself is twofold. First, any strong rudder movement tends to slow the boat down by creating turbulent water flow over the rudder. Second, as the boat turns, the rudder follows the original water flow for awhile. The stern doesn't follow the same arc as the bow because the center of rotation is near the middle of the boat. You can see this clearly in a calm harbor with no sails up and nobody holding the tiller. If you shove the bow to port, the stem goes to starboard and the tiller goes to starboard just as if you were on the port tack and were turning the boat into the wind. Since the rudder is following the water flow past the stern, it is obvious that in the beginning of the turn there is little or no drag caused by the tiller going to leeward.

The helmsman in a dinghy, on the starboard tack, is steering with his or her left hand using the tiller extension. As the boat turns and the tiller goes to leeward, the left arm extends. The helmsman then comes into the cockpit, swings the tiller extension aft, and crosses in front of the tiller, facing forward, with the left arm behind the back. As the helmsman gets over to the new windward side, he or she shifts to the right hand grasping the tiller extension and hikes out.

Meanwhile the crew has also shifted over to the new windward side. This shift of crew weight is sometimes delayed in order to tack faster through a maneuver called "roll tacking," most frequently used on dinghies. The theory is similar to trying to fly a kite on a windless day. As long as you are running with the kite string pulling the kite, it will rise up in the air. The forward movement creates a breeze and, in turn, this creates lift. When you stop running, the kite falls. Therefore, if we can swing the mast and the sails into the wind, they will stay full and create lift even if there is little or no actual wind. So as the boat turns, the crew hikes out hard, swinging the mast and sails up over them. The sails stay full of air even though the bow has passed through the eye of the wind. The crew then leaps across the boat and hikes out hard on the new windward side, swinging the mast back up toward the wind as the boat settles down on the new tack. Thus, the sails luff only for an instant instead of throughout the whole tack. Roll tacking is an extremely effective maneuver on small dinghies, but also works well on some larger boats. Be sure to check the racing rules about it if you are racing.

JIBING

Jibing without a spinnaker is a fairly simple process. The helmsman should bear off downwind until by-the-lee, watching carefully to avoid jibing accidentally. Then, after the proper commands, he or she initiates the jibe. The crew grabs all the parts of the mainsheet and pulls the main boom across. (This system of pulling all the parts of the mainsheet in a jibe makes the assumptions that the crew is experienced and that the boat sails like a dinghy, whether in light or heavy airs. On a larger cruising sailboat, the safe way to jibe is to pull the mainsheet through the blocks with turns on a winch to keep it under control unless the wind is very light.) In light air another crew member may pull on the boom vang to help the boom across. Just as the boom passes the centerline of the boat, the helmsman heads back downwind by pulling the tiller to the new windward side. This should negate the tendency for the boat to round up into the wind after a jibe. Even though the rudder is turned, the boat should sail straight. There are two reasons to pull all the parts of the mainsheet at once. First, the mainsail comes in four times faster (if the mainsheet is a four-to-one tackle). In light air this gives the boat a scoot forward, because it's like "pumping," which is explained later. Second, if you pull the line through all the blocks, their friction reduces the speed with which the mainsheet may be eased on the new side after the boom crosses the centerline. This, in turn, increases the wind power in the sail and enhances the tendency for the boat to round up into the wind, to broach. As in tacking, the helmsman should face forward at all times.

Figure 2-4. Wrinkles from the clew to the mast indicate the mast is over bent.

Figure 2-5. The small wrinkles along the luff can be cured by tightening the cunningham. Straighten the mast a little to cure the large wrinkles from the clew.

LIGHT-AIR SAILING

It has long been thought that one should have flat sails in heavy air and full sails in light air. However, many top sailors have come to recognize that a full sail is needed only when power is required, no matter whether the wind is light or heavy. In drifting conditions, it is conceded by most that one needs a flat sail.

When there is practically no wind, sails have to be set to maximize any puff that comes along. If there is a deep curvature in the sail, a puff is unable to attach itself readily to the lee side of the sail, since the airflow has to make too large a turn. A flat sail is, therefore, desirable in such conditions, for it doesn't require the air to deflect far from its normal direction to attach to the sail.

As soon as there's a breeze of 2 or 3 knots, full sails are required for low-speed power and acceleration. The racing sailor will start flattening the sails again at 10 or 12 knots of wind speed. A small sailboat that uses crew weight to stay flat may need to flatten sails earlier. A heavy keelboat sailing in heavy seas may need full sails up to a higher wind velocity. It all depends on the boat, the crew, and the wind and sea conditions.

In light-air conditions, be careful not to over-bend the mast or you will "turn the sail inside out." This occurs when the mast is bent more than the amount of luff roach that has been built into the sail. The visual result will be obvious by the wrinkles emanating from the clew (see Figure 2-4).

In purely drifting conditions, the cunningham should not be tensioned. It tends to pull the position of maximum draft forward, but does not flatten the sail. If you pull down hard on the cunningham in light air, the draft will go all the way forward and form a cup along the mast. Any puff hitting the sail is unable to make such a sharp bend, and will fail to produce adequate airflow to produce lift. However, you want to avoid the wrinkles near the mast, shown in Figure 2-5, caused by no luff tension at all.

In drifting conditions, in addition to having flat sails and light trim, you also must trim the sails as if you were close reaching. The boom should be leeward and never over the centerline of the boat because if a zephyr does hit the sail, the force is translated into leeway rather than forward motion. The jib should be led farther outboard than when there is a breeze. In light air you cannot "strap" the sails in. Doing so just slows the boat down.

The jib is played much the same way as the main in light air. A jib should have very light halyard and sheet tension, and little to no luff tension. In some cases, the jib sheet should be hand-held so its weight doesn't tighten or collapse the jib leech. A jib is shaped so that the clew is aft of a point directly below the head. When there is no wind to fill the sail, gravity causes the heavy clew to fall forward directly beneath the head. This cups the foot of the sail and tightens the leech. The effect is similar to releasing the outhaul of the main boom (see Figure 1-22). Holding the clew by hand will keep it from drooping forward.

Figure 2-6. Heeling the boat to leeward when beating in light airs to reduce wetted surface drag.

One of the most important things to remember is that once you can get a sailboat moving, its mass tends to keep it going even if the wind dies for a moment or two. Furthermore, as the boat moves, it creates an increased amount of apparent wind just by its own movement through the water. The cumulative effect of a little speed is amazing. Some large close-winded boats like 12-meters can sail extraordinarily fast in practically no wind at all.

But there are a number of hurdles you have to overcome in order to get the sailboat moving. One of the biggest is the frictional drag of the hull. You should be aware that every square foot of hull that is in contact with the water helps to slow the boat down. To reduce the amount of hull area that is in contact with the water, sailors sit on the leeward or low side and heel the boat to that side in light air as in Figure 2-6. Though a small amount of additional hull surface is immersed in the water on the lee side (mostly the topsides), much more of the underwater hull is lifted out on the windward side because of the rounded bottom. The net effect is a reduction of wetted surface, the amount of surface in contact with the water. The total result is reduced drag. There's an added advantage to heeling the boat to leeward. The boom will stay on that side of the boat because of gravity rather than flop back and forth, which knocks the breeze out of the sails. Because the boom stays in one place, so does the mainsail. This allows the main to fall into the shape the sailmaker designed into it. Thus, when a zephyr of wind hits the sails, they are all ready to do their work. The airflow passes over the already curved sides of the sails and results in drive. Without this heeling, the initial breaths of air have to shape the sails first before effective sailing can start. Of course, when breaths of air are few and far between, your boat may never get up to a sustained movement through the water, unless the sails are properly shaped to begin with.

Windage is another large detrimental factor in sailing to windward. To cut this down, the skipper and crew should stay as low as possible on the deck and bunch together to reduce exposure to the wind. Any mass attached to the boat that the air hits will slow down the boat's forward motion. Heavy thumping and jumping around the boat will also tend to slow it down.

The sails are operating at their greatest efficiency when the airflow is moving smoothly over the surface of the sail. And the same situation applies to water flow over the hull, keel, and rudder. And because the keel and rudder are lifting surfaces, any reduction in their efficiency causes the boat to make more leeway and also be slower to windward. So this is why, in drifting conditions, the crew should walk as though they were on eggs, and they should sit quietly and make all their movements slow and deliberate. On a boat with winches, you should use the winch handle to adjust the trim of a jib and do it by turning the winch click by click rather than manually pulling on the line. Any jerk of the jibsheet or mainsheet will disrupt the airflow over the sails.

In light air, a helmsman should hold the tiller or wheel very lightly in order to feel any slight tug put on the helm by the rudder. Though the helmsman should be sitting low in the boat, he or she must be able to see any dark patches on the water since this indicates a breeze. He or she must also develop the sensitivity to feel the direction of any slight breeze on the face.

When you are running before the wind in light or drifting conditions, you should again heel the boat. But this time you should do so to weather as in Figure 2-7. The crew in this photograph is not heavy, so the actual heel is rather slight. Nevertheless, note how the main boom is pointing up. What this does is lift the mainsail area higher off the surface of the water. Because every foot of increased altitude above the water surface means increased wind velocity, the mainsail now is in a stronger wind than it would be if it were not canted up at an angle. The increased velocity can be as much as 100 percent greater at heights of 35 feet than it is at two feet above the surface, though this does depend on wind strength.

Figure 2-7. Heeling the boat to weather helps speed on a run.

Of course, this heeling to windward also reduces the wetted surface, just as heeling to leeward does. It also reduces weather helm, which is undesirable when you are running, by submerging more of the weather bow and by getting the center of effort of the sail plan over the boat instead of out over the water where it can turn the boat to windward. And heeling to windward on a run also is good because it allows the spinnaker to fill, by gravity, out from behind the mainsail shadow, and this exposes it to free air that is undisturbed by the main. Obviously this is a solid benefit.

When there's very little wind, pumping the sails can help get your boat moving downwind. To do this you grasp all the parts of the mainsheet, or grab the main boom itself, and pull as hard and fast as you can toward the center of the boat. Then let the main go slowly out again, and then quickly jerk it in again. These rhythmic fanning jerks, done every few seconds, will propel the boat forward.

Rolling the boat, back and forth, will also help move it forward. To do this, stand up and, holding onto the mast and shroud, throw your weight as violently as you can from one side to the other. The mainsheet should be trimmed in tightly. This maneuver will be helpful only if there's absolutely no wind and you are beginning to despair about getting anywhere. Of course your boat must also be quite small.

While the crew is rocking the boat in the manner I have described, the helmsman can scull with the rudder. To do this, he or she pushes and pulls the tiller back and forth across the boat quite violently just as you would do with an oar. Surprisingly a pretty good turn of speed can be attained with this method. But don't try any of these rocking, pumping, or sculling techniques while you are racing (unless the race committee says you may) or you'll be disqualified. All of these techniques are against the yacht racing rules unless otherwise stated by the race committee.

If you have tried all these things and you still aren't getting anywhere out on the water and you're about to miss dinner, the only thing I can suggest now is to break out the paddles, start your engine, or hail a friendly motorboat for a tow home. And next time you probably should think twice about getting so far away from home if it looks like a light-air day.

HEAVY-AIR SAILING

The words "heavy weather" always are subjective. The wind that is a "nice sailing breeze" for a San Francisco sailor may be "heavy weather" for the sailor from Long Island Sound. For our purposes, though, let's call heavy weather a wind that is blowing over 25 knots with lots of white caps and streaks of spume on the water.

Most beginning helmsmen are apt to get tense in heavy air, probably because it's much like riding a skittish horse: you never know when or where you're going to be thrown. Try to force yourself to relax.

Always hold onto the wheel, tiller, or tiller extension with a firm, but not a tense grip. The latter is the "white knuckle" grip that often is used by less experienced sailors on windy days. If this tenseness is confined solely to your hand and forearm it's not a problem. However, the tense muscles do run right up into the upper arm and shoulder. This means that whenever the torso is moved, the tiller or wheel is as well.

On one of our school boats an instructor couldn't budge the tiller because the student's grip was so tight. Finally he had to move the entire body of the student to avoid a collision. This is an example of how the rigidity can be transferred. Always try to think that your steering arm is an independent part of your body. Grip the boat all you want with your other arm, but consciously relax your steering arm.

While you are beating on any sized boat, you should sit to windward in heavy air. It's common, on some keelboats, to see helmsmen sitting down in the cockpit to leeward in heavy air. The trouble is that he or she can't see the approaching waves from that position.

If the waves are running in the same direction as the wind (about 40–45° off your bow), the best way to play them is to head up, perhaps even pinch slightly, on the front side of the wave, then head off down the backside of the wave. This means you sail a short distance up the front of the wave when the wave's current or orbital flow is against you, and you traverse along the backside where the current is with you. This reverse flow on the backside of the wave will help push you to windward.

Figure 2-8. Don't tack in the trough of a wave. While the waves are small in this picture, you can tell by the splash to the leeward, that the boat has just fallen off the crest of a wave. Tacking would put the bow right into the next wave.

Figure 2-9. Tack at the crest of a wave, when the bow is out of the water.

With steep, short waves like the ones you can sometimes find in a current when it flows against a strong wind, heading off the wind at the crest of a wave also helps avoid the bone-jarring pounding that results from the boat literally falling into the next trough. Instead, it slides down the back of the retreating wave.

Unless a helmsman sits to windward, he or she is unable to see, and play, the waves, and this is a crucial part of heavy-weather sailing. And the helmsman will not be able to see the ripples of a gust on the water as it approaches. When a 35- to 40-knot puff hits, the force is substantial and, since the apparent wind comes aft, it will have even more effect on the helmsman who hasn't headed up to meet it.

Tacking can be very difficult in heavy winds. The main problem is the wind resistance of the rigging, the flapping sails, and the resistance of the hull to the seas. If the boat isn't traveling fast to begin with, a skipper attempting to tack may end up in irons, head to wind and dead in the water. The wind and seas will quickly stop the boat, making the rudder useless. To avoid this, be sure you have adequate speed. Wait for a relatively calm spot (both wind and sea, if possible) before you attempt to tack. Tack at the crest of the wave when much of the bow and stern is out of the water. Less hull in the water means easier pivoting. It's very much like a skier making his turn on a mogul or mound of snow, when the ends of the skis are in the air.

Though the photos are not taken in heavy air, the boat in Figure 2-8 has just fallen off the crest of a wave as you can see by the splash to leeward. To tack at this point will put the bow right into the next wave to come along. The boat in Figure 2-9 is tacking as they go over a wave. Note the bow is out of the water. When conditions are very rough and you have to be sure of completing the tack because of some obstruction, have your crew delay releasing the jib sheet. Let the jib back momentarily when you tack, but do so just long enough for the wind to help push the bow over to the new tack.

Running downwind in heavy weather can be wildly exciting and more than a little tense for any new helmsman. In such a situation it helps to think ahead. Think about the worst that can happen, then say to yourself that even the worst isn't so terrible, so why worry about little things like being out of control, jibing wildly, broaching, etc. If you've ever had the "worst" happen, as I have, you'll know that it's all pretty quiet after you have lost a mast or you capsize. It's the wild speed and commotion short of the worst that scares you. If you think about it in those terms, you'll perhaps find yourself even enjoying being at the very edge of control.

One major problem for the novice helmsman (and even for some who are experienced) when running in heavy winds and seas is oversteering. The seas toss the boat around, threatening to jibe it one way, and broach it the other. An already tense helmsman tends to overcorrect. By this I mean he or she still is steering in one direction when the boat already has changed its course to the same direction. For example, a boat may be swinging to starboard and the helmsman will steer to port to counteract the swing. But the boat then starts swinging to port before the helmsman has a chance to reverse the helm. The helmsman is trailing the boat's gyrations and actually reinforcing them.

The solution to this problem takes a strong will in the beginning, but it will become more natural and instinctive with some experience. The way to beat this is to try not to steer. Yes, I mean don't move the tiller or wheel more than a few inches either way. Probably at first you will steer horribly. But soon you will find that with proper anticipation and a good, hefty shove at just the proper time, very little rudder action is really needed. The boat won't sail in a perfect straight line, but in heavy seas you can't expect it to. You are, however, going to be sailing a much straighter course than one where you are using a lot of rudder.

Another requirement for a good heavy-weather downwind helmsman is surfing know-how. If the wind is so heavy that it precludes "pumping" (rapid trimming of the sails), the only way a boat can get up and stay on a surf is by good helmsmanship. To do this takes practice. But as a large wave approaches from astern, you should head up toward a reach to pick up speed—just like a surfboarder paddles furiously in front of a wave. When the stern starts to lift, head down the wave. The trick is to aim your bow for the lowest part of the trough in the waves ahead. If it looks like you are going to overtake the wave ahead, start traversing the wave. When you lose the wave, keep an eye out astern for the next good one. When you see it coming, first head up for speed, then head down and start riding it.

Heavy-weather helmsmanship takes practice, just like everything else. But if you shy away from sailing on heavy days, you'll never know how to handle such winds when you're caught out in them inadvertently. You'll never know whether your boat and crew can take it, and you'll never know how you will tackle the unusual problems that arise. You'll soon find that heavy-weather sailing gives you a nice feeling of accomplishment when you come ashore at the end of the day.

WINGING THE JIB

Before we get into spinnaker work, let's talk about winging the jib, carrying it on the windward side of the boat, opposite the main. There are times when we find it safer and less work to wing out the jib with the spinnaker pole, particularly in heavy winds. Release both jib sheets. Grab the windward jib sheet forward of the jib lead block and snap the pole jaw over it. Push the pole forward to the clew of the jib. Slide the pole straight forward just to windward of the headstay. Don't try to push the pole to windward, just forward. When you have reached the inboard end of the pole, still holding the pole and jib sheet at the same time with one hand, reach up and snap the inboard jaw into the ring of the mast. That done, keep tension on the jib sheet and grab the sheet aft of the jib lead block with the other, taking in the slack. Then release the sheet and trim normally.

To properly trim a winged-out jib, pull the pole back as far as possible without letting the leech of the jib collapse or fold over. The leech of the jib should act like the luff. When it "luffs," let the pole forward. A topping lift and foreguy are not necessary because the clew of the jib will hold the pole up as long as the jib sheet is tight. The pole should be level or pointing downward. The higher the ring on the mast, the more the pole points down and the more pressure there is on the leech of the jib. In other words, if the top part of the leech is twisting off, snap the pole into a higher eye on the mast to correct it.

Once the jib is properly trimmed, steer by it. If you head too high, the leech will fold over. If you head too low, the mainsail may jibe. A boom preventer, a line from the end of the boom to a cleat on the foredeck will prevent an inadvertent jibe.

TEST QUESTIONS

1. Does heeling to windward increase or decrease weather helm on a run?
2. What is "roll tacking"?
3. Should you tack at the crest or the trough of a wave in heavy air?
4. What is "wetted surface"?
5. What is "pumping" a sail?

Balance and Apparent Wind

A well-balanced boat will tend to maintain its heading when you release the tiller, and a stable boat can absorb more force of wind in its sails without heeling excessively. The greater the ability of a boat to stay upright, all else being equal, the faster it will go. A stable boat is sometimes called a *powerful* boat.

BALANCE

To sail properly, and certainly to race successfully, you must always consider a boat's balance. By "balance" I mean the tendency of a boat's heading either to deviate to the side or to continue in a straight line when the helmsman releases the tiller or wheel. If he or she lets go of the tiller and the boat turns away from the wind to leeward, the boat is said to have a "lee helm." Conversely, if the boat turns to windward, it has a "weather helm." If it sails straight ahead, the boat is balanced.

Though these are useful guidelines, be careful not to be misled by what I call "artificial" weather helm. A boat will normally turn into the wind when the tiller is released. Because of the forces acting on the rudder's windward side, "lift" is generated due to the angle of attack with the water flow. If the rudder post is located on the leading edge of the rudder and attached to the trailing edge of the keel, all the area aft of the post is pulling to windward, which tends to turn the boat into the wind.

Separated or "spade" rudders are now standard on most boats, large and small. The rudder is usually placed near the stern where it can have maximum steering leverage. These rudders usually are "balanced" in that the rudder post is located on the rudder about one-fourth of the way back rather than attached along the leading edge. Hopefully, the center of pull to windward in this case is at the post and the rudder, therefore, and will remain straight. Balancing the rudder this way reduces artificial weather helm. It also decreases true weather helm because the rudder, as a lifting surface, pulls the stern of the boat to windward a small amount.

Excessive leeway can also cause artificial weather helm. Take an extreme example of a boat with no forward motion that is slipping straight sideways through the water. The water on the leeward side of the rudder behind the rudder post will push the rudder blade to windward, giving the appearance of weather helm.

The way to distinguish artificial from true weather helm is to deter-

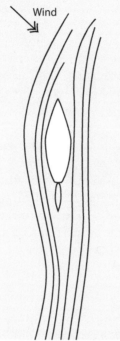

Figure 3-1. The rudder is attached to a skeg or to the trailing edge of the keel.

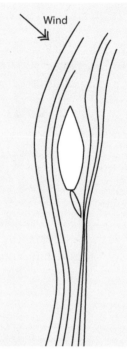

Figure 3-2. A small amount of weather helm adds lift and reduces leeway.

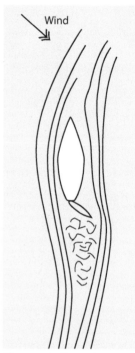

Figure 3-3. Excessive weather helm causes turbulence and drag.

mine whether the rudder must be deflected from the centerline in order to make the boat sail straight. If the tiller or wheel must be cocked a few degrees to windward to make the boat sail a straight line, it does have true weather helm.

I've sailed on cruising boats with balanced spade rudders where the owners swore they sailed fastest with a "neutral" helm, and that once they had developed a slight weather helm, the boat slowed down. However, my observation showed me that although the helm "felt" neutral (there was no tug on it because the rudder post entered the rudder well aft of its leading edge), he did indeed have a slight weather helm because the tiller was being held to windward a few degrees. But when the helm was increased to a point where the helmsman could actually feel it, there was a large enough rudder angle to slow the boat down by creating rudder drag.

When sailing to windward in most boats, a little weather helm is desirable. If the rudder is attached to the trailing edge of the keel, as in Figure 3-1, it is obvious that a couple of degrees of rudder used to counteract a slight weather helm will force the water to follow a greater curve on the windward side of the keel. (See Figure 3-2.) This gives the keel "lift" and reduces leeway. However, too much weather helm will cause turbulence and drag as shown in Figure 3-3.

The same principle applies with a spade rudder, which gets its lift from the angle of attack the rudder makes with the water. A little weather helm cocks the rudder to windward, increasing the angle to attack, and thereby increasing lift.

A really well designed boat should have a slight weather helm, which will increase as the wind velocity increases. Because weather helm creates "lift" for the rudder, it also gives the helmsman a "feel" for the boat. The slight tug on the tiller (or wheel) allows the helmsman to ease pressure on the tiller and let the boat come up even closer to the wind.

Increasing pressure on the tiller makes the boat fall off away from the wind. In other words, the helmsman really only needs to steer in one direction; the boat steers itself in the other. If a boat has to be steered toward the wind as well as away from the wind, it is said to have no "feel," and the boat becomes, in fact, extremely difficult to steer.

Another very important reason to have some weather helm is that a boat will automatically head up in a puff. Heading up reduces heeling, and it also maintains the angle the wind originally made with the sails because the apparent wind has come aft. In short, a small amount of weather helm is almost a built-in device to improve your sailing.

APPARENT WIND

The sidebar (page 30) covers the basics of apparent wind. Apparent wind angle changes when the true wind direction changes, but the boat speed and wind velocity remain constant. To carry this a step further, let's change boat speed and wind velocity, keeping the true wind direction as a constant.

Figure 3-4 shows a boat sailing close-hauled on starboard tack with

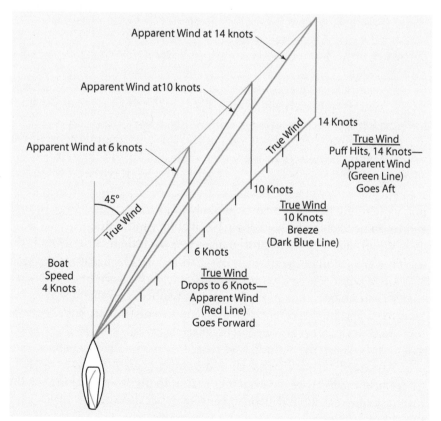

Figure 3-4. Apparent wind comes aft in a puff and forward in a lull.

APPARENT WIND

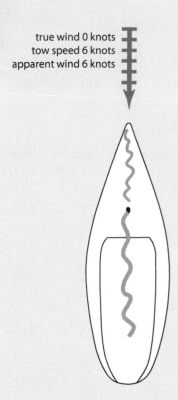

true wind 0 knots
tow speed 6 knots
apparent wind 6 knots

Towing a boat on a dead-calm day creates apparent wind dead ahead.

Another type of shift, which also causes the need for sail adjustment, is a change in the apparent wind direction. While true wind is what your masthead fly and telltales show when your boat is not moving through the water (at anchor or docked), apparent wind is what you feel and what you see in your telltales and masthead fly when the boat is underway.

Apparent wind is derived from the combination of wind produced by the boat moving through the air and wind produced by nature (true wind). Cigarette smoke, telltales, and electronic wind-direction indicators all indicate apparent wind direction when you are moving.

Imagine that you are standing up in a convertible on a windless day. As the convertible starts forward, you begin to feel a breeze on your face that increases as the speed of the car increases. This is like boat speed wind. At 10 mph, you feel a 10-mph breeze on your face. This is apparent wind.

Now imagine yourself in the same parked car, pointing north with an easterly wind (true wind) of 10 mph. You feel that wind hitting the right side of your face. As the car starts forward you don't feel two different winds—one on the side and one on the front of your face. You feel a resultant wind coming from an angle forward of the true wind. This is apparent wind.

The illustration at left shows apparent wind when towing a boat at 6 knots on a dead-calm day. Since there is no true wind, a resultant angle is not produced and the apparent wind is coming from dead ahead at the same speed as the boat: 6 knots. On your first day out on a close-hauled course, you may wonder why the telltales on the shrouds indicate you are almost sailing directly into the wind, while you are technically sailing around 45° off the wind. The telltales are indicating your apparent wind—the resultant angle of your boat's forward motion and the true wind.

You can demonstrate the force and direction of apparent wind by drawing a parallelogram on graph paper, keeping your boat's speed and the true wind in the same scale. The accompanying art shows a boat close-hauled,

the true wind 45° off the bow. Boat speed is four knots and the true wind speed ten knots. Let's see what happens when a puff hits.

The extension of the true wind line to 14 knots indicates a four-knot increase in wind velocity. When we work the solution out graphically, we learn a basic axiom: "In a puff the apparent wind angle will come aft."

To be absolutely correct, this would apply only if there were constant boat speed throughout. However, if the increase is just a puff, by the time the boat picks up speed the puff will have passed, so the axiom is essentially true.

We already know that we should point higher in a gust in order to reduce heeling. Now we have another reason to do the same thing. As the gust hits, apparent wind will go aft causing more heeling, less drive, and a

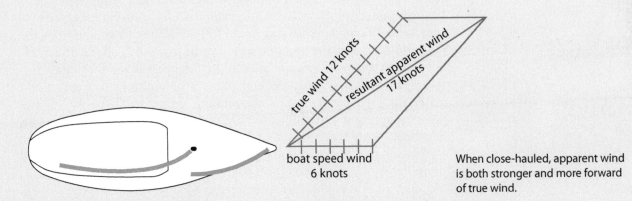

boat speed wind
6 knots

When close-hauled, apparent wind is both stronger and more forward of true wind.

sailing at 6 knots in a 12-knot true wind. Suppose you know your boat tacks in an 80° arc (the distance it will travel when moving from one tack to another). Therefore, the true wind direction is at half of your tacking range, or 40° off your bow. To find the strength and direction of the wind you feel—the apparent wind—draw a parallelogram on the graph paper using your boat speed (6 knots) and the true wind (12 knots). Then draw a diagonal line through the parallelogram. The diagonal line measures 17 knots of apparent wind by your scale. Now, using a protractor, the apparent wind reads 27° from your heading (versus 40° for the true wind). This demonstrates that on a close-hauled course, the apparent wind is greater than true wind strength.

There are four points to remember about apparent wind:

1. The strength of apparent wind lessens as true wind comes aft.
2. Apparent wind is always forward of true wind, unless true wind is dead ahead or astern.
3. When true wind is well aft, a small change in true wind direction makes a large change in apparent wind direction.
4. When on a beam reach or close-hauled, apparent wind is of greater velocity than true wind.

changing angle of incidence (the angle the apparent wind makes with the sails). The net result is that the sails are now improperly trimmed unless you head up or ease the sheet or traveler.

This particular change in apparent wind direction is very important, especially on light days. If you have a three-knot breeze, the wind velocity in a puff is apt to more than double the regular breeze. If it is blowing 15 knots, a gust may get to only 20–22 knots—only a third higher. Therefore, the movement aft in apparent wind direction is often greater on light days than it is on heavy ones.

The red line shows the resulting change in apparent wind if it suddenly dies. With boat speed remaining constant and the wind velocity lowering to six knots, the apparent wind will go forward. One way for the novice to remember this is to imagine the wind dying completely just as though someone had switched off a giant fan. Obviously, in the absence of any wind, the only breeze you would feel would be that produced by the forward motion of the boat and would come from dead ahead. So any reduction in true wind velocity must bring the apparent wind forward.

This happens quite often on light days, particularly to large cruising boats that have a great deal of momentum. The sails will start luffing and give the appearance of sailing too high or too close to the wind. Actually, the boat is only traveling through a light spot or "hole" in the wind. The helmsman must make an immediate decision: Is it a valid wind shift, called a header, or is it just a hole? If it is the former, he or she must head off to fill the sails. If it is the latter, he or she could kill what little speed there is by heading off instead of shooting through the light spot with momentum and picking up the breeze on the other side.

It's always a difficult decision to make unless you can see a puff ahead. Usually the wisest course is to head off very slowly and evenly. If you're still luffing after turning 20° away from the wind, it's probably a flat spot.

One warning: A skipper who reacts precipitously and turns the boat quickly downwind actually aggravates the situation if it's just a hole in the wind. The turn itself forces air against the lee side of the jib, causing it to luff or back. In short time he will find himself 30° below his previous course, but the jib is still luffing because of the turning movement of the boat.

Of course, it may not be a hole, but rather a true header (the wind shifts toward the bow). The boat is sailing a straight course in a light, steady breeze and suddenly, because of the wind shift toward the bow of the boat, the jib starts to luff. The skipper decides that instead of heading off to fill the sails, he or she will tack. As the bow turns into the wind, the jib will fill as the apparent wind comes aft, due to the turning of the boat. Because the jib has stopped luffing, it can appear that the wind has shifted back to its original direction. The skipper can have the impression that the boat has been lifted (the wind direction has changed more toward the stern of the boat) when actually it is only the pivoting of the boat that has caused the change.

An inexperienced or indecisive skipper will stop his tack in the middle and return to his original course. At first it will appear that he or she has made the correct decision because, by making the incomplete tack, the boat has slowed, which puts the apparent wind fairly well aft. As the boat picks up speed, the apparent wind will again come forward and the boat will be sailing in the same header as before.

Now consider cases where wind speed remains constant but boat speed varies. For instance, if the boat starts surfing down the face of a wave (much as the surfboarder would use a wave), the apparent wind goes forward to the point where it can flatten a spinnaker back against the mast and rigging.

At times the boat may slow down for some other reason. As the apparent wind comes aft, its velocity will increase. As the wind velocity doubles, the pressure on the sails and rigging quadruples. When a boat runs hard aground at high speed, it is often dismasted because the rig and sails have a tendency to keep on going even though the hull has stopped. But another important reason is that the apparent wind pressure on the sails has increased suddenly.

A good example of this happened to *Mare Nostrum*, a 72′ yawl, on the 1955 Transatlantic Race from Cuba to Spain. We had a spinnaker, mainsail, mizzen (the small sail on a yawl's aftermast), and a mizzen staysail (sort of a jib for the mizzen mast) set in fairly fresh winds of about 20–23 knots. The swivel on the spinnaker halyard broke, and the chute went out ahead of the boat. Before we could get it aboard, it filled with water, went underneath the bow, and hooked on the keel. This slowed the boat down so suddenly that the top half of the mizzen mast toppled forward under the increased load on the mizzen staysail.

So always remember that whenever there is a change in either boat speed or direction, or wind velocity or its direction, there must also be a change in apparent wind. A helmsman must be alert to it and either change his course accordingly or the crew must trim or ease the sails. Also remember that the force of the wind on the boat varies as the square of the speed. For instance, the square of a 10-knot breeze is 100. The square of a 12-knot breeze is 144. That's a 44% increase in wind force with just a two-knot increase in wind speed.

TEST QUESTIONS

1. What is chord? Draft?
2. What does the traveler do?
3. Does backstay tension "cock" or "free" the leech of the main?
4. Does raking the mast effectively move the jib lead forward or aft?
5. What is "turning the sail inside out"?
6. Should the sails be full or flat in heavy airs and large seas?
7. What is a "balanced" rudder?
8. What happens to the apparent wind in a puff?
9. What happens to the apparent wind when a boat suddenly surfs?

Spinnaker Work

The spinnaker adds a great deal of sail area and power to almost any size boat. It is a challenge to achieve smooth, trouble-free spinnaker work, but there is great satisfaction when the challenge is met. After you've flown a spinnaker a few times, the task will become easier, and the result will be pure pleasure at the added speed.

WHEN TO FLY IT

First, you must always make a decision whether or not to fly the spinnaker at all. Is the wind too heavy or light? Is the wind too far forward of aft? Is the crew experienced enough? Usually these questions are interrelated. For instance, some spinnakers can be carried to advantage when the apparent wind is well forward on light to medium days (as close as 55° to 60° relative from the bow), but they would cause weather helm and possibly broaching (rounding up and heeling out of control) at the same apparent wind angle on heavy days.

The wind strength and direction weigh heavily on the choice of types of chutes, as they are often called (short for "parachute" spinnaker). There are close-reaching, reaching, and running chutes. The former are flatter in cut and made of heavier cloth, while the latter are fuller and lighter. Some boats use asymmetrical spinnakers, which are designed to be used without a spinnaker pole. We will get to these later in this chapter.

Another factor in deciding whether to fly the spinnaker or not is its sail area relative to the jib. On some boats the jib is quite large, and if you find the wind too far forward or heavy enough to cause broaching, you may find the boat will go faster without the spinnaker. On others, the spinnaker has so much more area than the jib that even if you are broaching with it up, you will probably net out with a faster speed through the water. If you are racing, go by the old axiom: "When in doubt, set." If cruising or daysailing, the reverse is the best advice: "If in doubt, don't set."

On very heavy days it almost always pays to carry a spinnaker downwind if you're racing. I've heard the argument on cruising boats many times that if the boat is already at hull speed, setting a spinnaker won't improve boat speed. That's fallacious reasoning because in a trough of a wave and up the other side, the boat is rarely going near hull speed, and it needs the extra power of a spinnaker. And under surfing conditions, there is no such thing as hull speed, for all sailboats can surpass it. The spinnaker will give just enough more power to start the surf earlier and make it last longer.

On very light days a chute can be set, and will fill well, if the spinnaker cloth is light enough and the apparent wind relatively far forward. But with the wind aft, particularly with leftover slop rolling the boat around, a jib may do just as well. The spinnaker will just flop back and forth, wrapping around the headstay and catching on the spreaders. You're often better off without it in such conditions.

THE SET

Now, how to "get the damn thing up." Ever hear these words before? Let's assume we're sailing a small one-design keelboat with a three-man crew. Pretty much the same procedures are involved in both larger and smaller boats; they just have more or fewer people.

A spinnaker is a triangular sail made of nylon. The two vertical edges are called luffs when the sail isn't set because the spinnaker is symmetrical and both edges are identical. When the spinnaker is set, the edge leading up from the pole is the luff, and the other edge is the leech. The edge along the bottom is called the foot.

Some potential problems can develop before the boat even leaves the mooring. If the spinnaker is improperly packed, it can get twisted as it is hoisted. Most spinnakers are packed in sail bags, buckets, deck depressions, or other containers. Most are commonly called spinnaker turtles because the container originally used was a piece of plywood covered by an old inner tube, secured along three edges, under which the spinnaker was stuffed. Placed in the bow, this object looked like a turtle and the name stuck.

To properly turtle a spinnaker, find the head of the sail. Usually it is the only corner of the sail with a swivel. Grab one luff near the head and follow down the edge of the sail flaking it back and forth. After you have followed down one side of the sail, change hands and follow down the other side to the clew, flaking in the same manner. Mark the location of the head with a finger lest it get lost in the folds of the sail. Then, still holding on to both edges, stuff the spinnaker into the turtle.

The three corners of the sail should be on the top of the bag or container, and should be separated. If a sail bag is used, the three corners are usually tied together with the head between the tack and clew. This will work 99% of the time, but sometimes the three corners get a 180° twist so that the tack and clew are reversed in relation to the body of the sail. The spinnaker might rotate itself out of such a potential wrap, but if the wrap tightens up, it will be the devil to get out.

One of the best ways to picture how you set up for a spinnaker is to imagine a slow-motion movie of a spinnaker being hoisted, run backward. In other words, from out and drawing, the spinnaker will collapse and slowly fold itself back into the turtle. Imagining this will show that all sheets and halyards must be outside all shrouds, jib sheets, barber haulers, etc., in preparation for the set. In Figure 4-1 a crew attached the halyard to the clew and hoisted it upside-down.

Figure 4-1. Upside-down spinnaker set.

Study Figure 4-2 and learn the various lines involved in spinnaker work.

The afterguy, more commonly the guy, runs through the pole, which is always set out to windward opposite the main boom. The free corner of the spinnaker has a sheet attached to it like any other sail. The only tricky thing about the foregoing terminology is that during a jibe, the pole is switched over to the new windward side and the old sheet becomes the new guy (running through the jaws in the end of the pole).

There are two lines to hold the pole in position—the topping lift to keep it from falling when the spinnaker isn't full of wind, and the foreguy (some people call it the spinnaker pole downhaul) to keep the pole from "skying" (pointing way up in the air) when the spinnaker is full.

The most common error I've run across is the failure to make a last-minute check to see that the spinnaker halyard is clear. It must be outside of everything. It is too late to discover that the halyard is inside the topping lift, fouled around an upper shroud, or was led between the jib halyard and jibstay when the spinnaker is halfway up and filling.

As the wind increases, there's a point where a spinnaker can over-power the boat if it's used at its maximum effectiveness. The choice then is to either reduce the effectiveness of the spinnaker or change to a jib. The former is often the best choice. To reduce a chute's effectiveness, ease the pole forward and down, and overtrim the sheet. Make sure the spinnaker halyard is two-blocked—hoisted as high as it can be. Then lead both the guy and sheet farther forward to pull the sail down and to partially blanket it by the mainsail. Trouble usually results when the spinnaker gets out too far into fresh undisturbed air.

When reaching, the sheet lead should also be forward of the transom if the spinnaker is short along the foot. With the lead aft at the stern, trimming the sheet to stop a curl just stretches the foot. If the lead is brought forward, a pull on the sheet will uncurl the luff, and if the spinnaker is designed well, it won't tighten the leech. A tight leech must be avoided on a reach because it creates a drag to leeward and backward.

SPINNAKER TRIM

There is no mystery about what makes a crew member a good spinnaker trimmer. It's experience and concentration, and neither of these can be taught. One is developed, and the other innate. We can teach the basic rules of spinnaker trimming, but it is up to the person to become good at it.

Even the basic rules can be misleading. Nothing is hard and fast in sailing, and for every rule there's an exception or two. First, let's examine the general principles behind spinnaker trimming. When running, there's a little flow around the backside of the luff (from a crew member's vantage point), but that doesn't result in much drive. Therefore, we want the greatest projected area possible. Projected area is the area on a flat plane that is presented to the wind.

Just as a large parachute will let a man down more slowly than a small one, the more area of spinnaker exposed to the wind, the greater its effec-

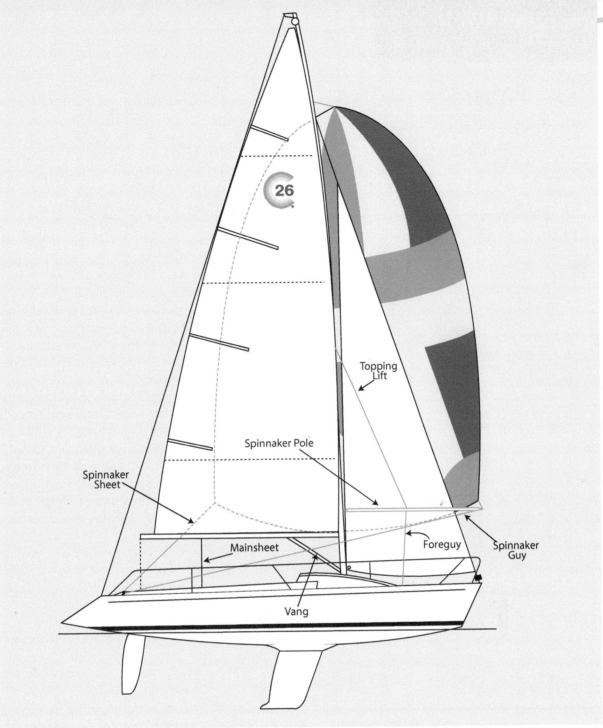

Figure 4-2. The lines and controls used in spinnaker work.

tiveness. This is done by keeping the pole well squared (aft) and the sheet well trimmed.

If there weren't a price to pay for having the pole well aft, that's where we'd set it, but there is. As we square the pole aft, and also trim the sheet to keep the spinnaker from collapsing, it is drawn in closer and closer to the mainsail. This means that the spinnaker is in the bad air of the main and loses efficiency. So we ease the pole forward and ease the sheet to get the chute away from the sail plan. Somewhere there is a happy medium between starving the spinnaker behind the main and losing projected area through too much ease, and this is where experience comes in.

The next general aspect of spinnaker trimming to remember is that a

Figure 4-3. A distorted spinnaker can be caused by improper pole height and reduce efficiency.

Figure 4-4. Fairly tight slot betweeen luffs of jib and spinnaker but a little halyard ease has helped.

spinnaker is a symmetrical sail and should look symmetrical when flown. Although there are a few exceptions to this, such as when close reaching or in light air, it is generally true. If the spinnaker is misshapen, as in Figure 4-3, because the pole is too high or too low, it will lose much of its effectiveness. Keeping the above two general aspects of spinnaker trimming in mind, all the rest of the basic rules fall in place.

Following are some of the requirements for pole position. A good starting point is to set the pole square to the apparent wind. The masthead fly is in undisturbed air and is a good guide. Set the pole at right angles to it. As the boat sails farther downwind, however, air over the main tends to flow forward and around the mast, making the spinnaker practically by the lee. This means that the pole will need to be squared back, past perpendicular to the masthead fly. Actually, it will be perpendicular to the shroud telltales. I would use the masthead fly until the wind is well aft and then switch to shroud telltales.

There are some unusual cases where the masthead fly isn't very accurate for spinnaker trimming, such as on a 12-meter yacht. Being a ¾ rig, the head of the spinnaker is considerably lower than the masthead fly, and the apparent wind at the top of the mast is noticeably farther aft than that at pole height, due to increased wind velocity aloft. Another exception to setting the pole perpendicular to the apparent wind is when you are using a very short footed spinnaker. In that case, squaring the pole brings the clew near the jibstay and much of the projected area is lost.

The pole should generally be level and perpendicular to the mast, not necessarily parallel to the water. This means that if you raise or lower the outboard end of the pole, you should raise or lower the inboard end (the end attached to the mast) a corresponding amount. The idea is to get the spinnaker as far away from the sail plan as possible, but constant adjustment of pole level can do more harm than good. A pole has to be cocked 25° from the level to decrease its effective length 10% and during the first 20° only 5% is lost, so a few degrees off of level really doesn't make much difference. Probably more is lost by fussing around with inboard pole height than is gained by having the pole exactly level. Also, a slight cock upward will put the pole in line with the guy and reduce the bending strain on the pole.

More important is the height at which the whole pole is set. The general rule is to keep the tack and clew of the spinnaker level with the plane of the deck (not with the water). But this really goes back to keeping the

Figure 4-5. Raising the pole opens the slot for the boat to leeward.

Figure 4-6. Ease the sheet until a curl appears along the luff, then trim.

Figure 4-7. This spinnaker is "starved" for air. The sheet should be eased, the pole squared, or both.

spinnaker symmetrical. When the two corners are level, the spinnaker is symmetrical, looks good, and flies well.

The exceptions to this occur mainly while reaching, and in either high or low wind velocities. While reaching, particularly when flying the spinnaker with the jib set, the tack of a normal reaching spinnaker on a class boat can be set higher than the clew. This opens the slot between the spinnaker and the jib. It also eases the luff of the spinnaker and flattens the chute. Figure 4-4 shows the tack and clew fairly even. There is little space between the jib and spinnaker luffs. The pole on the right-hand boat in Figure 4-5 is quite high and the slot is open, but the spinnaker is a bit misshapen. With a flat spinnaker designed for tight reaching, the reverse is true. The tack (the pole end) should be set quite low, and the luff set like a genoa on a pole.

Once the pole is set correctly, it's fairly simple to play the spinnaker. The sheet should be eased until one sees a slight curl along the luff as in Figure 4-6, and then trimmed to make the curl disappear. This must be done constantly and is where concentration plays its biggest part. Quite often the novice overtrims the spinnaker, which gets in the disturbed air behind the mainsail and collapses as in Figure 4-7. This is called a "starve." Pull the pole aft to correct the problem.

The spinnaker guy should also be played if you are running in a slop. As the boat rolls to windward, the pole must be squared and the sheet eased. As it rolls to leeward, the pole should be eased forward and the sheet trimmed.

All changes in apparent wind direction necessitate changes in pole position and sheet trim. If the boat starts surfing, if it falls off a plane, or if

39

the wind velocity changes, the apparent wind direction will be affected and the spinnaker trimmer will have to make adjustments. Moreover, he or she must learn to anticipate these changes and be ready to act.

HALYARD EASE

There are times when one should ease the spinnaker halyard, but when is it good to ease it off—and how much?

The next time you are on a reach with the spinnaker set, look up behind the mainsail on the lee side. Then ease the spinnaker halyard 6 inches or so while looking at the leech of the sail, not the head. It will become obvious how much the slot between the spinnaker and the main will open up to allow free air passage.

When running downwind in a breeze, easing the halyard has two effects. First, it gets the spinnaker away from the disturbed air of the mainsail, and second, it allows the spinnaker to be more vertical than it is when fully hoisted. In light air, however, the halyard shouldn't be eased, since the spinnaker will just come straight down. Nor should it be eased on a reach in heavy air, because the sail's center of effort will go farther out over the water and possibly cause a broach. On a run in heavy air, an eased spinnaker will be more apt to roll from one side of the boat to the other (oscillate) than one fully hoisted. In short, easing the halyard is rarely done on a run and is really only beneficial on a medium air reach.

LIGHT-AIR SPINNAKER WORK

Spinnaker trimming in light air takes a great deal of patience. Lower the pole way down, but always keep the pole end a little higher than the clew. Then, when a puff of air comes and fills the spinnaker, the pole will be at the proper height. In other words, keep the pole at the proper height for the 10% of the time that the spinnaker is filled and doing the boat some good, not the 90% of the time when it is drooping and not producing any forward drive. Another reason to keep the pole a little higher than the clew in light air is that a low pole will stretch the luff and fold it over (see Figure 4-8). When a puff arrives, the spinnaker is unable to fill because of the shape of the luff.

The same thing can happen with some very full-shouldered running spinnakers. The luff can collapse from a starve, and though you know you must pull the pole aft, first you have to overtrim the sheet to unfold the luff. Only then can you pull the pole back with the spinnaker full. It is better in light air to have the pole too low rather than too high, as this causes the spinnaker to droop to leeward and it will need a much stronger puff to fill it.

Another light-air problem is caused by the jib.

Figure 4-8. An excessively low pole tightens the luff and causes the spinnaker to collapse more easily.

Air flowing past the lee side of the jib causes a suction on a reach, and if the spinnaker collapses, it sucks into the jib and is very difficult to fill it again. The natural tendency is to trim the jib to get it away from the spinnaker, but actually the opposite should be done. The first time the spinnaker collapses, free the jib sheet to break down the airflow over the jib. If it happens a few more times, take the jib down or roll it up.

JIBING THE SPINNAKER

Spinnaker jibes seem to be a great bugaboo for most crews, but they don't have to be. Though almost any crew can get into trouble, sometimes it is very difficult to analyze the problem. A jibe happens fast and all crew members have tasks to perform. When you're busy with your own job, it is often hard to notice where things are going wrong. Most of the time the person on the foredeck who is all wrapped up in spinnaker cloth, lines, etc., is the butt of abuse when actually the fault lies with the person steering.

The skipper who turns the boat too sharply and gives the crew inadequate time or directions will almost certainly cause a bad jibe. In heavy air, the helmsman must be sure to counteract the tendency for the boat to round up into the wind right after a jibe. The boom swings over with a great deal of force and, when it reaches the end of the mainsheet, it stops abruptly and the sail creates a wall to the wind. Something has to give until an equilibrium is found, so the boat heels over and a strong weather helm results. The forces in the sail out over the water turn the bow of the boat toward the wind. This combination of factors will cause a broach in heavy winds unless the helmsman heads the boat off decisively to meet the anticipated turning moment. Done properly, the boat, though being steered as if to jibe back again, just sails straight ahead. Nothing can make a crew look worse than a bad helmsman.

Reach-to-Reach Jibe

But, to be fair about this, some of the worst problems are caused by the crew handling the spinnaker guy and sheet. A "reach-to-reach" jibe is one in which the boat is turned from a reach with the pole near the headstay on one tack to a reach with the pole near the headstay on the opposite tack. It is a difficult type of jibe because the boat is turned approximately 90°. The spinnaker has to get completely around to the other side, and problems occur if this is not done with alacrity.

As the boat heads down from the starboard tack reach in order to jibe, the pole should come aft and the sheet should be eased (Figure 4-9). After all, the boat is on a dead run at the instant of jibing, and the spinnaker should be trimmed properly for downwind sailing as in Figure 4-10. The jibe of the main boom and spinnaker pole is then completed, and the boat heads up to the new port tack reach. The pole should be near the headstay and the sheet trimmed in. In Figure 4-11, nothing of the sort has happened. At the point of jibing, the spinnaker is still on the port side of the boat, the same side as the wind is about to come over. After the jibe, the spinnaker starts to blow through between the headstay and the main.

Figure 4-9. Preparing for a reach-to-reach jibe.

Figure 4-10. At the point of jibing, after squaring, the pole is taken off.

Figure 4-11. The skipper jibes too fast and the spinnaker fills between the mast and the headstay.

Figure 4-12. The skipper heads downwind and fills the sail while the foredeck crew snaps the pole on the mast.

Figure 4-13. During a jibe, foredeck crew faces forward with back braced against mast.

When this happens, about the only solution is to head back downwind to blow the spinnaker forward around the jibstay as in Figure 4-12.

During the jibe, the foredeck crew on a boat like the Colgate 26 pictured here should stand, back against the mast, facing forward, as in Figure 4-13. From this position, he or she has much more leverage for controlling the pole and getting it off the mast. Also, they can see the spinnaker and help keep it full. On a reach-to-reach jibe, they should take the pole off the mast and then off the old guy. This makes the spinnaker free-wheeling, and the mid-cockpit crew can pull the spinnaker around the boat without the pole restricting it in any way. The foredeck crew then connects the end of the pole that was previously on the mast to the new guy and snaps the other end of the pole onto the mast fitting. This is called "end-for-ending" the pole.

When the pole is not taken completely off the spinnaker, the foredeck crew has to be extremely quick not to end up in the situation shown in Figure 4-14. The crew here decided to snap the end that came off the mast on to the new guy before unsnapping the pole from the old guy. The cockpit crew has pulled the spinnaker around to the starboard side, but cannot pull it any farther because the pole is against the shrouds. The jibe has been completed, and the spinnaker is starting to blow in between the headstay and the main. If the pole were not attached, the spinnaker could have been pulled all the way around to the starboard side even if the foredeck crew was having trouble getting organized.

Running Jibe

A running jibe is much easier. The boat's heading changes only slightly, so all we are basically doing is changing the pole from one side to the other while keeping the spinnaker full. Figure 4-15 shows a running jibe at midstage. The foredeck crew is in a good position, back braced against the mast and feet spread apart for balance. In light winds as shown, the skipper holds the main boom in the middle of the boat for a short time to keep the spinnaker full while the pole is being transferred to the other side. In the case of a running jibe, the pole may be left attached to the old guy until the other end is snapped over the new guy. Thus, the foredeck crew can help keep the spinnaker full during the jibe. Figure 4-16 is taken at the point when the jibe is almost completed. The foredeck crew has the pole on the new guy and is attaching the other end to the mast.

End-for-End Jibe

The end-for-end jibe is used on small boats with a light spinnaker pole. The person on the foredeck stands behind the pole facing forward (Figure 4-17A, page 44). Just before the jibe, the foredeck crew disconnects the pole end from the mast and from the guy (B) at the same time. As the boat turns downwind, he or she grabs the sheet and snaps the jaw of the pole over it. Then the pole is passed across the boat and the free end attached to the mast (C). Meanwhile, the person in the cockpit is easing the sheet and trimming the guy as the boat turns into a jibe. This keeps the spinnaker downwind and full of air. The skipper pulls the main across and, if the wind is blowing hard after the boom crosses the centerline, he or she turns the boat back downwind to keep it from broaching (rounding up broadside to the wind), which it has a tendency to do after a jibe.

Dip-Pole Jibe

A dip-pole jibe is used on larger racing boats where the pole is too heavy or awkward, making it dangerous to disconnect completely from the mast. Raise the inboard pole end on the mast, trip the pole end out of the guy, lower the pole end to pass through the headstay, connect the lazy guy, and raise the pole end to level at the same time as lowering the inboard pole end to level.

Figure 4-14. Foredeck crew should have disconnected old guy before jibing. Now the pole, which cannot be seen in this photo, is against starboard shrouds and spinnaker cannot be pulled farther around the headstay.

Figure 4-15. A running jibe at midstage.

Figure 4-16. A running jibe almost completed.

Figure 4-17. (A) The start of an end-for-end jibe. Detach the pole from the mast first. (B) Next detach the pole from the guy and attach the end of the pole to the old sheet. (The line that was the sheet becomes the spinnaker guy.) (C) Attach the pole to the mast to complete the jibe.

DOUSING THE SPINNAKER

Taking a spinnaker down to leeward is quite simple—the only major problem is caused by letting it get out from behind the mainsail into strong, unobstructed wind. The crew gathering in the chute must have control of the sail by bringing the sheet forward to a spot just behind the shrouds. The guy is then eased and the halyard lowered, as the sail is pulled in behind the mainsail. If someone lets the guy go before the sheet is under control, the chute will go flying aft to the stern and will be the devil to gather in.

There may be times when a windward douse is in order. If you plan to set the spinnaker again and the next set is on the other tack, a windward take-down will prepare you properly for the next set. On windy days a windward take-down also avoids having to send a crew to leeward to grab the sheet.

Take the pole down before you intend to douse (Figure 4-18) and then just pull the spinnaker around to windward with the guy as the halyard is lowered (Figure 4-19). Many smaller boats set and douse the spinnaker to windward as a matter of course.

COMMON SPINNAKER MISTAKES AND PROBLEMS

There is only one sure way to avoid problems with the spinnaker—don't set one. But if you don't, you'll also lose almost all of the pleasures of sailing a boat on a

Figure 4-18. Windward spinnaker douse: Get pole out of the way first and fly by hand.

run. There are certain procedures that will minimize problems and others that will solve them faster.

For instance, the crew in Figure 4-20 is able to get their spinnaker "sea anchor" aboard more easily because the skipper has turned the boat right into the wind. The boat stops and the water pressure filling the spinnaker disappears. Or, if they can't get the boat to turn into the wind, they should pull on just one corner of the spinnaker, so it can be brought aboard without water resistance. The following are some other common problems—and the easiest ways to solve them.

Halyard Raising

Figure 4-21 shows what happens if the halyard is not clear all the way up before hoisting. When the topping lift was attached to the spinnaker pole, the halyard was between the pole and the topping lift. Either lower the halyard and untangle it, or disconnect the topping lift from the pole, let it go, and grab it again after the spinnaker has filled. Always make a last-second check before hoisting to make sure that the halyard is clear all the way up.

Figure 4-19. Windward spinnaker douse, continued: Then gather the spinnaker in to windward pulling on the guy.

Wraps

This problem plays no favorites. Even large cruising boats with crackerjack crews can get spinnaker wraps. They happen when the spinnaker collapses for one reason or another and starts to rotate around itself. Wraps can also occur as the spinnaker is hoisted if the corners of the spinnaker are not pulled apart quickly enough or if the bag has been inadvertently rotated before the set. When the wrap is very low in the spinnaker, it probably has to be lowered and sorted out. Never pull the pole back or head the boat up

Figure 4-20. A sea anchor is dragged astern to slow the boat down during storms. It's usually a canvas bag (like a windsock) not a spinnaker, as above.

Figure 4-21. Spinnaker halyard caught under the topping lift.

in order to fill the spinnaker on the assumption that the wrap will unwind if the spinnaker is full. It doesn't work and, in fact, makes the wrap tighter. Get the spinnaker in the dead air behind the main and jib and "blanket" it. Then shake it or pull down on the leech. The wrap shown in Figure 4-22 should come out with this method. If the wrap is high in the sail, releasing the halyard a few feet would allow the swivel, which may be jammed in the block, to rotate and unwind the spinnaker.

A bad wrap is one in which the chute winds itself around the headstay. If it gets tight, it can be next to impossible to unwrap without cutting the spinnaker away. If the boat has a wire headstay, the wire has strands that are twisted around each other. As the spinnaker is pulled down (assuming a crew member can reach the foot of the sail), it is rotated by the strands and gets tighter and tighter. Once a headstay wrap occurs, jibe the main boom so the airflow off the mainsail is in the opposite direction. Instead of wrapping tighter, the spinnaker starts rotating in the opposite direction and unwrapping itself. I've known of this method for many years but never had to resort to it. A few years ago, however, one of our teaching boats developed a tight spinnaker wrap around the jib while running in a 25-knot wind. Nothing seemed to work, so we suggested (from a chase boat) that the crew jibe the mainsail. Within minutes this "impossible" wrap had completely unwound itself.

The type of wrap shown in Figure 4-23, which is low in the spinnaker and wrapped around the headstay, probably is incurable without lowering the spinnaker and starting anew. The crew appears to be despairing.

Losing the Guy and Sheet

Often both the guy and sheet get free inadvertently. It sometimes happens during a jibe when one person is holding on to both and the spinnaker suddenly fills with a gust of wind. More often, it happens on the douse. The guy is released before someone has a hold on the sheet behind the mainsail on the leeward side. The sail goes flying out, as in Figure 4-24. One solution is to turn the boat dead downwind. In all but the heaviest winds, the spinnaker will come down within reach and can be gathered in. Another solution is to pull on just one line, either the guy or the sheet, and let the other trail free. As the corner gets close, ease the halyard. Premature halyard ease, however, runs the risk of having the spinnaker fill with air way out beyond the boat as shown here. When this happens the problem becomes serious. The boat may be pulled over so far that she fills with water, and the heeling makes it impossible to turn the boat "into" the spinnaker (i.e., downwind) to relieve the pressure. Freeing the halyard completely, or cutting it, may become necessary. An obvious solution to the problem, stop knots in the end of the spinnaker, guy and sheet, is an absolute NO-NO! Far worse problems can result from such knots.

Figure 4-22. A typical spinnaker wrap.

Figure 4-23. A very difficult wrap to solve.

46

Figure 4-24. Someone released the guy and sheet prematurely.

Premature Filling

Another common problem is having the spinnaker fill with wind before it is all the way up. On a small boat this can cause a capsize, and on a larger boat, it may be difficult to raise the rest of the way because of the strain on the halyard. If the spinnaker fills prematurely, head directly downwind to blanket it behind the mainsail.

Losing the Halyard

Premature ease of the halyard before another crew member is prepared to gather it in, or inadequate securing (cleating) of the halyard after the spinnaker is raised, can cause the problem shown in Figure 4-25. If this halyard isn't caught and brought back up immediately, the spinnaker will either fill with water or be run through by the bow of the boat. Easing the halyard on the douse faster than it can be gathered in leads to the problems experienced by the crew in Figure 4-26. The chute is about to fill with water under the bow, the weight of which will inevitably wrench the rest of the spinnaker from the grip of the crew. All this could have been avoided if the person easing the halyard had watched the person gathering and had tried not to get ahead of him or her.

SPINNAKER BROACHING

No matter what size sailboat you sail, if you set a spinnaker in heavy air, you will probably broach at one time or another. Fifteen-footers broach and 80-footers broach. Size is no deterrent.

A mild form of broaching is shown in Figure 4-27. It is essentially an overpowering weather helm caused by a number of factors. When the weather helm (the tendency for the boat to round up into the wind) becomes so strong that the helmsman is unable to counteract it with the rud-

Figure 4-25. Halyard slipping can cause major problems.

Figure 4-26. The crew on the halyard eased faster than the spinnaker could be gathered in.

Figure 4-27. A broach.

der, the boat will broach. Most of the time this means that the boat will just wallow broadside to the wind until steering control is regained and the boat can be headed back downwind.

A major factor causing broaching is heeling. As mentioned before, excessive heeling causes a tremendous weather helm as the bow wave pushes the hull to weather. The helmsman has to steer the boat well to leeward to keep sailing straight.

Contributing to additional weather helm is the fact that the force in the sails is out over the water when heeled. Let's fantasize for a moment. Imagine that in Figure 4-27 we have tied a line around the mast just above the spreaders and have run it all the way to shore where we've tied it to the back of a car. Now, we drive the car inland pulling the mast faster than the hull of the boat can keep up. By looking at the photo and using your imagination, it should be clear that first the boat will rotate until it is parallel to the shore, and then the car will be dragging the whole mess shoreward by the mast. The hull at this point will be dragging sideways through the water, creating such resistance that the mast will be almost lying in the water from the pull of the line.

With the spinnaker out over the water, the total wind force affects the boat in exactly the same way as our imaginary line to the shore. The more the boat rotates into the wind, the more it heels, until we have a full-fledged broach on our hands.

In a broach, the rudder becomes next to worthless. The boat is lying on its side, so the rudder is near the surface where it can't get a "bite." Since the rudder is more parallel to the surface than vertical and perpendicular to the surface, steering to leeward has much the same effect as the elevators on the tail of an airplane. The stern and keel will lift rather than turn. So the more the boat heels, the less effective the rudder becomes in turning it back downwind to reduce the heel. In fact, the rudder will start to increase the heel after a certain amount of heel is reached.

If, in the early stages of a broach, the helmsman is able to turn the boat so that the hull is parallel to the direction of pull (on our imaginary line to the shore), the hull has less resistance and a better chance of keeping up with the sails. In other words the helmsman should try to steer the hull of the boat under the rig, keeping the mast as vertical as possible. The tendency to broach will be reduced. To facilitate catching the broach before it develops, the skipper and crew can take certain precautions.

Since heeling is the enemy, they must hike out hard during gusts of wind that could precipitate a broach. Another way to reduce heeling is to luff the sails. Since the spinnaker gives the boat a great deal of drive, it is the last sail to luff. First, luff the mainsail. Remember—if your boom vang is on tight, the boom is being held down. As the mainsheet is eased, the boom end goes into the water and is pushed back toward the center of the boat. Since the main can't be eased, more heeling will occur and the boom will be pushed even closer to the hull by the water flow. This will cause even more heeling and another vicious cycle starts, until a broach occurs. So, ease the boom vang. In fact, many racers disregard the mainsheet and play only the boom vang to avoid a broach. The boom lifts as the vang is eased, and the top part of the sail, near the head, luffs first. Since this is the part that causes most of the heeling, the sailor is reducing heeling without detracting much from the general drive of the sail.

The next sail to ease is the jib, if one is being used under the spinnaker. It is fallacious to think that trimming the jib will reduce weather helm by blowing the bow to leeward. Whatever lee helm could develop by this method is nullified by the weather helm caused by the additional heeling of the jib when trimmed tightly.

When it is obvious that drastic measures are needed to avoid a broach, the spinnaker can be collapsed by easing the sheet a couple of feet. The helmsman must anticipate the need for this and give the command to the spinnaker trimmer to "break" the spinnaker. When the boat has been steered back downwind and has straightened up, the spinnaker can be trimmed again to fill it.

There are a few other factors that can contribute to broaching. If the spinnaker halyard has stretched or is not all the way up, the center of effort of the spinnaker (its "pull") will be farther out over the water and aggravate the turning moment. The tack of the spinnaker should be right at the end of the spinnaker pole for the same reason. If the pole is too high, the luff will have a large curve to leeward, causing the drive to be farther out over the water. And if the leech of the spinnaker is cupped rather than flat and free, the trapped air will cause more heeling.

Crew weight should be aft on reaches for two reasons. First, the forward force on the sails against the resistance of the hull will have a natural tendency to bury the bow and lift the stern. This tendency is pronounced in many catamaran designs when reaching. They tend to bury the bow of the lee hull and actually "trip" over it (capsize). The crew has to move way back near the stern of the weather hull. Second, crew weight aft keeps the rudder deeper in the water and increases its effectiveness.

ROLLING OR OSCILLATING

Figure 4-28 shows another problem in spinnaker work: rolling, or oscillating. The boat in the photo is rolling by the lee and will shortly roll in the opposite direction. In heavy seas this can become wildly exciting. Your boat is almost jibing as the mast rolls to windward, nearly broaching as it heels to leeward. Most of the problem is caused by allowing the spinnaker too much freedom.

In the photo, the sheet has been eased to the headstay (hidden from view) so the spinnaker is able to get completely around to the starboard side of the boat. It then pulls the mast over in that direction. As it heels, the starboard bow wave develops and shoves the bow to port, toward a jibe. The helmsman steers the boat hard in the opposite direction; the spinnaker oscillates over to the port side of the boat, causing heeling and a strong weather helm, which, again, the helmsman counteracts. Thus the rolling starts. If there is any ease in the halyard, the spinnaker is free to spin in a large arc. Pulling the halyard up very tightly reduces the rolling.

Off the wind in heavy air, the mainsail becomes a large factor in control, particularly on small boats. A powerful boom vang is a must. If the boom is allowed to lift in the air, the top of the leech will fall off so far that it may actually point forward of abeam, or at least be folding over the spreader and shrouds. Figure 4-29 is a cross section of the mainsail near the foot and another cross section near the head. Note that while the foot of the sail is stalled, the top part of the sail is getting airflow over the lee side, creating lift in the direction of the arrow. This tends to pull the top of the mast to windward, making the boat roll to windward. Once started, each subsequent roll is a little more severe. The apparent wind goes more forward and flow is picked up lower down in the sail each time the mast rolls to weather, and the faster it rolls, the more forward the apparent wind goes. The more forward the apparent wind goes, the greater the area of mainsail that develops airflow on the lee side, and the greater the lift. The greater the lift, the faster the mast swings to windward, and so on, until the boat is rolling madly. The solution is to vang down strongly and, if the vang can't handle the forces, to trim the mainsheet in a little so the top part of the sail is also stalled. Though the vang in Figure 4-28 appears to be fairly tight, we can see by the spreader poking into the mainsail that the top part of the sail is well forward of the bottom, so more vang and mainsheet tension would be helpful.

When rolling conditions exist, consider hoisting or unfurling the jib, then trimming the jib in flat. It will help to keep the bow downwind and help dampen the rolling like a baffle. Changing course to more of a reach can also help. Further, in such conditions we want to reduce the effectiveness of the spinnaker. By easing the pole forward of square with the apparent wind and by overtrimming the sheet, we can roll part of the spinnaker in behind the mainsail, thereby partially blanketing it. This also keeps the spinnaker from picking up airflow on the lee side, which, like the main, pulls the spinnaker over to the weather side of the boat and rolls the mast to windward. Lower the pole to keep the spinnaker in closer to the sail plan of the boat, but don't overdo it. Lowering the pole excessively on a

Figure 4-28. Rolling by the lee.

running chute makes the luff fuller in cross section and more likely to collapse. In heavy winds the jolt of the spinnaker filling after having been collapsed can easily break something. Make sure the pole foreguy is tight so the pole can't swing back as the boat heels to windward. Never let the tack of the spinnaker fly out beyond the pole end, as in Figure 4-30. It can cause wild rolling.

Place your crew weight on opposite sides of the boat as in Figure 4-28. Just as children can seesaw faster if they're closer to the middle of the seesaw than when sitting at the very ends, the boat will roll less if the crew weight is spread out wide apart. And, last, change helmsmen if it appears that the current one doesn't quite have the anticipation or timing to counteract the rolling.

As with all sailing, don't accept problems such as broaching and rolling as unavoidable. Certainly, they can happen to any crew, but you should work at reducing the problem to more acceptable and manageable terms.

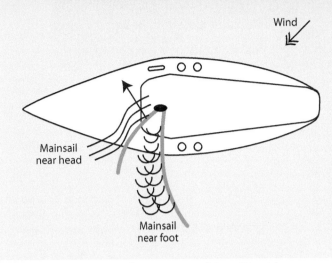

Figure 4-29. Twist causes the upper part of the sail to pick up airflow and aggravates rolling.

ASYMMETRICAL SPINNAKERS

You can use asymmetrical spinnakers on almost any sailboat. We have used them on Colgate 26 sailboats, and often yachts over 100' LOA use them. Their effectiveness depends on whether the boat is designed for them or designed for a symmetrical one. To use them effectively when racing, the

Figure 4-30. A spinnaker flying out beyond the pole. Note, this is against the racing rules. The tack of the spinnaker must be in close proximity to the pole.

boat needs to be high-tech enough to sail sufficiently fast on a reach to offset the extra distance sailed by reaching back and forth, whereas a symmetrical spinnaker can be used effectively well downwind (see the polar diagrams in Chapter 5). A boat that is designed for asymmetricals will normally have a pole, either retractable or fixed, extending in front of the bow of the boat that the tack line runs through. This gets the spinnaker well in front of the bow, and it can be jibed easily in front of the headstay. It also moves the sail away from the sail plan, and allows the spinnaker to fill with wind better.

Boats that do not have such a pole will set an asymmetrical, often called a "gennaker," mainly as a large reaching sail as shown in Figure 4-31. Since no spinnaker pole is used, it is easier to set and jibe, and fewer crew are needed. The spinnaker is often contained in a "snuffer," a cloth sleeve. You connect the tack line to the tack and the sheet and guy to the clew. Then you pull the snuffer on a clothesline-type halyard up to the head of the sail and it's set. To douse, you head downwind, blanket the spinnaker behind the mainsail, and pull down the sleeve.

TRIMMING ASYMMETRICAL SPINNAKERS

Let's say you have one set at the end of a pole. When you are reaching, you want it to look a lot like a genoa, so the tack is pulled down low and the luff is pretty straight. As you head downwind, you ease up the tack and let the spinnaker rotate to windward. If the tack line tends to leeward instead of being vertical or tending to windward, you have eased the tack too much and it needs to come back down. Keep the luff on the edge of a curl. A few inches of curl are best. Too much curl reduces the sail's power. To get the spinnaker to rotate to weather out from behind the mainsail, heel the boat to windward, just as with the symmetrical spinnaker in Figure 2-7 (page 22).

JIBING ASYMMETRICAL SPINNAKERS

There are two types of jibes, an outside jibe where the clew flies forward of the boat and sail and an inside jibe where the clew is pulled through between the headstay and the luff of the spinnaker. The former is easiest when the tack runs up from a block in the bow of the boat and there is little space for the sail to jibe forward of the headstay. The latter is easiest when the tack is on a pole extending forward a substantial distance from the bow. In either case, it's like jibing a jib: ease the leeward sheet and trim in the windward one. In both cases, if it is not blowing too hard, keep the mainsail temporarily amidships so the wind can keep the sail full.

Figure 4-31. An asymmetrical spinnaker used for cruising is called a "gennaker." Note the "snuffer" near the mast and the tack set near the bow.

There is one other way if you are cruising and short-handed: pull down the snuffer to douse the sail, set it up on the new jibe, and raise the snuffer back up to set the sail in the new jibe.

TEST QUESTIONS

1. What's the last thing to do before pulling the spinnaker up?
2. Should you head up to fill the sail when you have a wrap?
3. If the spinnaker collapses with a jib set, what should you do about the jib?
4. What does easing the spinnaker halyard do? When should it be eased?
5. To help avoid broaching, should crew weight be forward or aft?
6. If the spinnaker halyard is eased a little, will rolling be more aggravated or more controlled?
7. In light air should the spinnaker pole be lower or higher than the rest of the sail generally?
8. Should the foredeck crew face forward or aft when jibing the spinnaker?
9. If you are on port tack and the next set will be on starboard, should you take the spinnaker down to windward or to leeward?
10. What is "projected area"?

Chapter 5

Polar Diagrams

To get the best performance out of your sailboat, you should have a basic understanding of VMG (velocity made good) and polar diagrams.

We know that sailboats on different points of sailing move at different speeds in the same wind strength. A boat sailing upwind usually sails slower than a boat on a reach. If we're sailing to a destination upwind, the boat with the best VMG (speed directly upwind) will get there first. Look at Figure 5-1. Boat A has dropped out of the race, turned on the engine and is powering directly upwind at 5 knots. Boat A's VMG is 5 knots. Boat B is continuing to race and is close-hauled at 45° to the wind direction and is also sailing at 5 knots. If we draw a line over to Boat B's course perpendicular to the wind direction, we see that boat B is sailing only 3.3 knots

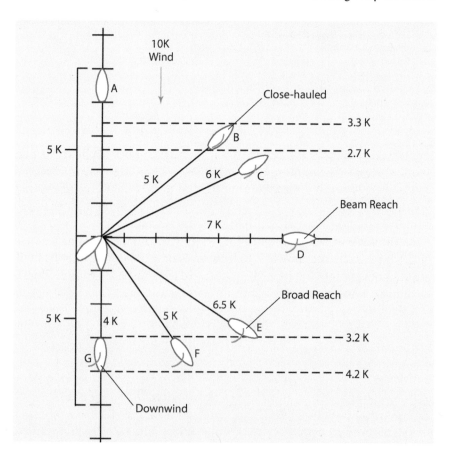

Figure 5-1. Sailboats, even when all in the same wind, will sail at different speeds depending on their point of sail. This illustration shows boatspeed variations in a 10-knot (10K) wind.

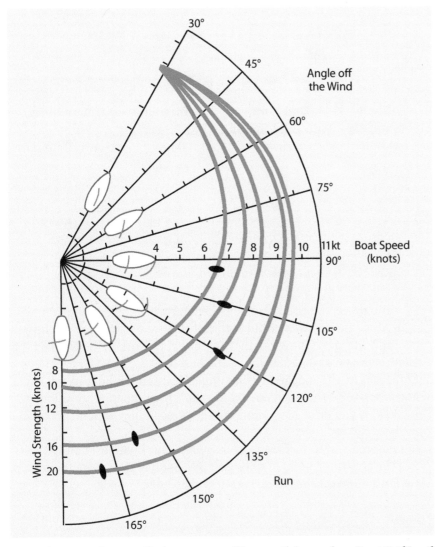

Angle off
the Wind

Boat Speed
(knots)

Wind Strength (knots)

Run

directly upwind. Boat C's skipper says, "I can sail faster than Boat B if I sail about 15° lower." He or she gets the boat up to 6 knots by sailing lower, but the result, when you draw the perpendicular line, is Boat C is sailing only 2.7 knots upwind. Boat D is sailing a beam reach, the fastest point of sail, but is making no progress upwind or downwind.

The same works for boats sailing downwind. Boat E is sailing very fast on a broad reach, but its VMG to leeward is only 3.2 knots. Boat F is sailing 1.5 knots slower, but its VMG to leeward is almost a knot faster. Boat G is sailing directly downwind, but only at 4 knots, because it's a slow point of sailing, but is getting to a destination downwind faster than the others.

If we connect the bows of these hypothetical boats, we get a curve which is the position of each boat in 10 knots of wind depending on the angle to the wind they're sailing. This is a polar diagram.

Normally, a polar diagram will show curves depicting boat speed at various wind strengths for a particular boat. In Figure 5-2 the wind strength curves are at 8, 10, 12, 16, and 20 knots and show the optimum speeds for a 54' sloop both beating and running. The solid boats depict the optimum run angles as taken from the table that follows.

BOAT SPEED AS A FUNCTION OF TRUE WIND VELOCITY AND APPARENT WIND ANGLE

Wind Strength (knots)	Optimum VMG Beat Speed (knots)	Optimum VMG Run Speed (knots)	Optimum Run (Apparent Wind) Angle
8	4.415	4.753	94°
10	5.015	5.707	102°
12	5.397	6.471	122°
16	5.800	7.774	159°
20	5.970	8.657	168°

The curves are calculated on either true wind angle or apparent wind angle. Since the apparent wind is that which we feel and see on the boat as it sails, the apparent wind angle is easiest to work with in polars. For instance, the polar diagram shows the best downwind VMG for 10 knots of breeze is at 102° apparent wind angle. Just sail the boat so the apparent wind is 102°. This is taken directly from your apparent wind indicator or "AWI." If you don't have wind instruments, judge the angle from your masthead fly.

To obtain a performance package for your boat, just call US SAILING, the governing body of sailing, at 401-683-0800, or write them at PO Box 1260, 15 Maritime Drive, Portsmouth, RI 02871-0907.

TEST QUESTIONS

1. What is "VMG"?
2. Which is easier to use when working with polar diagrams, true wind angle or apparent wind angle?
3. What is an "AWI"?

Basic Racing

Racing is both cerebral and physical. We'll try to take care of the cerebral part in this book. The physical part is practical experience on the race course. The differences between individuals will be not only how well they master each separately, but how well they can combine the two. I've known sailors who can really make their boats go. If you sail alongside them, they leave you behind. But during a race they inevitably make some strategic or tactical blunder that causes them to finish way back. I've known others who are rules experts, tactical experts, and really know their theory. However, they are so uncoordinated and inept on the boat that other boats pass them right and left on the race course. Combine the good qualities of the two, and we have a sailor who is practically unbeatable.

Since the first thing you'll encounter when racing is easily the most important, most critical, and most stressful situation, we'll begin at the beginning.

THE START

Most races use a standard starting sequence of signals over a five-minute period. A warning sound (a gun or a horn) is fired and a class flag is raised. One minute later a second sound is made, and the "P" for "preparatory" flag is raised. It's a blue square with a white square in the center. Three minutes later a third sound is made, and the preparatory flag is lowered. One minute later is the start when the class flag is lowered and a sound made. To reiterate, the first sound at five minutes before the start is the "warning" signal. Four minutes to the start is the "preparatory" signal. One minute before the start is the one-minute signal and then comes the start. These are important insofar as you are technically "racing" from the "preparatory" signal. In other words, if you foul a boat or touch a mark or have your engine running after the "prep," you're in trouble. When I was young I used to use a little memory aid for these signals that may be helpful in the beginning. "Water Polo" reminds you that the "warning" is followed by the "preparatory."

Remember that the gun or horn or whatever your Race Committee uses is a device to draw attention to the signal. There is nothing official about the sound device. If it misfires or is early or late, that's tough. It's the flag or the shape that counts, and the exact timing for a signal depends on the instant that the flag hits the top of the hoist or is broken out. Since the gun is fired when the flag reaches the top, if you don't hear the sound, start your watch when you see the flag.

Be sure to assign specific duties to the various crew members. The smaller the number of crew, the more duties each has to assume. The singlehanded skipper, of course, has to do them all. Typical of such duties are: (1) spotting potential collisions and right-of-way boats, (2) calling the time remaining, (3) judging how close to the line you are, (4) sail trim, (5) noting any last minute wind shifts, (6) potential tactical problems like a competitor overlapping your lee quarter, and (7) whether you are being called back by the committee for being over the line early.

Added to this list of duties are what I call "input considerations." These are facts that the skipper should know that will have a bearing on his start, such as: (1) wind direction, (2) wind type, (3) which end of the line is favored, (4) how long it takes to run the line, (5) current, and (6) the course to the windward mark. Let's go into more detail about both the duties and the input considerations.

CREW DUTIES DURING A RACE

Collisions and Right-of-Way

The crew doing the calling needs to have a good 360° view of all the surrounding boats. On most boats it is not important to hike out over the side until just before the starting gun on the final approach. So he or she may be able to crouch in the cockpit if the boat is large enough, and be able to see to leeward. On cruising boats a lookout is often posted in the bow before a start. Weight in the bow is very detrimental to the speed of the boat, though, so he must get aft quickly after the start. He should not distract the skipper with a constant barrage of boat locations, but only tell him about boats that could be a potential hazard. Even though you have right-of-way, don't relax your vigil, because you can be disqualified along with the other boat under the rule "a boat shall avoid contact with another boat if reasonably possible." The most common rules that come into play before the start are "a port tack yacht shall keep clear of a starboard tack yacht," "a windward yacht shall keep clear of a leeward yacht," and "a yacht clear astern shall keep clear of a yacht clear ahead."

Timing

Watch for the shape to go up and start your watch when it hits the top of the hoist. Sometimes it's hard to see the shape. If so, take the time from the smoke that comes from the gun, if any. It will take a little time for the noise to reach you, so don't rely on the sound of the gun for your timing. The skipper should make every attempt to place the boat in a position for the timer to get an unobstructed view of the shape. He or she should never be far away from the Committee Boat and should never be in the process of tacking or jibing about the time a signal is expected to be raised, broken out, or lowered. Such a maneuver takes the timer's attention away from his job. Since the sails of competitors can obstruct the view of the signal and since most boats sail back and forth to leeward of the Committee Boat (when the first leg is a beat), a good position to get the time on is upwind of the Committee Boat to one side or the other (not in front of its bow).

It's best, in a boat with two or more crew, to have two stopwatches timing the start in case one is stopped accidentally. Often skippers can improve their judgment of the approach by glancing at their own watch rather than just hearing the seconds remaining being called out by a crew member. Don't buy the type of watch that hangs around your neck. One that straps to your wrist is far better because it's not bouncing around hitting things. Also you don't have to fumble to find it. When the time remaining is being called out by a crew member, it should be done clearly and succinctly in half-minute intervals until the last half minute before the start. Then "20 seconds," "15 seconds," "10 seconds" and "5-4-3-2-1 start" should be called out.

Timing the start has a great deal to do with the type of boat you're sailing. If it's a light boat that accelerates rapidly, you can just about sit on the line luffing your sails and trim them in just before the gun. Catamaran sailors do this all the time. If you're racing a heavy, displacement type of boat it will take a long time to get it sailing at top speed, so you can't afford to slow up much as you approach the starting line.

A good method for timing the latter is known as the "Vanderbilt" start. Cross the starting line going away from it on a reach and note the time remaining. ADD to it the amount of time it should take to complete the tack or jibe to return toward the line. Divide by two and the result is the time remaining your watch should show when you start your tack or jibe. For example, your watch shows a minute and 20 seconds remaining as you cross the line going away. It takes you 12 seconds to tack. This totals 92 seconds (80 seconds plus 12 seconds). When your watch shows 46 seconds to go (92 seconds divided by 2), start your tack to start back to the line. You should arrive on the line at the gun. This method was derived by Commodore Vanderbilt for the enormous J-boats used at that time in the America's Cup. These boats sailed close-hauled almost as fast as on a reach. Plus, they were match racing (only two boats) so the wind was not being broken up by other boats. In practice nowadays, one has to allow a little extra time for the approach to the line since modern boats reach much faster than they beat and also, in fleet starts, boats to windward of you will interfere with your wind and slow the boat up on the return to the line.

Judging the Line

If the starting line is a long one and you intend to start near its middle, it's very difficult to judge accurately when you are right on the line. Skippers in this situation tend to play it cautiously with the result that there's apt to be a big sag in the middle of a long starting line of boats (see Figure 6-1).

You can minimize your loss by sailing beyond the buoy end of the line and lining up on the buoy and the starting flag on the Committee Boat with any convenient landmark ashore, such as a rooftop or a tree, providing, of course, there is land in that direction.

It may be possible to get a range from the Committee Boat end, but

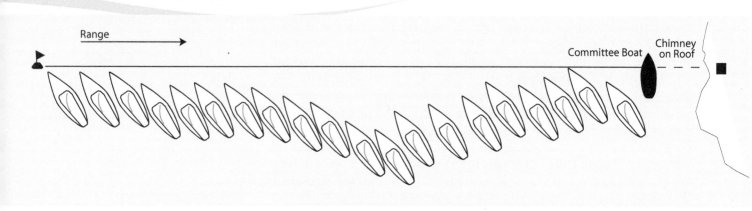

Range

Committee Boat

Chimney on Roof

Figure 6-1. Boats lined up along the starting line, note the "sag" in the middle of the line.

often the boat blocks you from getting a good view of the buoy and the land. This range should not be taken too early, because the Committee Boat may shift position, or a change of current may cause it to swing, which would change the range.

As you are approaching the line to start, watch the starting flag on the Committee Boat against the shore very carefully. As you approach the line, the starting flag will move along the shore toward your landmark. (See Figure 6-1.) If they line up just as the gun goes, your bow will be over early, because of your physical position in the boat when you noted the range. So hang back slightly from lining them up at the gun.

In one International 14 regatta I sailed, I found, using this method, that the sag in the middle of the line was two boat lengths of open water between us and the other starters. You will have a decided advantage over the other boats starting in the middle of the line if you can get two boat lengths ahead of a bunch who think they are getting a perfect start or even feel they might be early.

One Finn dinghy sailor I know decided to play for starting line sag even though there were no landmarks to confirm it. He started ahead of the boats in the middle of the line each race of a big regatta, and never was called back for being over early! That's playing it risky, though, because I've found many times the sag just isn't there.

I've found another way to judge the location of the starting line in boats like a Soling, a 27-foot keelboat sloop, open cockpit, weighing about 2,200 pounds. (I've sailed a number of championships and the 1976 Olympic Trials on Solings.) If there's no chance for a range, lean way out over the side of the boat to windward. Look forward and aft at the two ends of the line as you are running along it. Sitting on the rail, it might appear you are right on the line. But when you lean way out, the perspective changes and you can see how far from it you really are.

Sail Trim

Before the start large adjustments in speed are necessary. We're not thinking about the fine nuances of sail trim. It is crucial that the skipper states clearly exactly what he wants. If he or she wants to slow down he or she may say "kill it," whereupon the crew will let the main and jib luff. If the skipper wants to stop dead, he or she will probably say "back it," meaning to back the main against the wind. If he wants to accelerate rapidly, he'll probably say "trim for speed."

Many skippers concentrate their practice on accelerating the boat, but very few practice what is equally important: stopping the boat. When you back the main hard on the leeward side, it usually gives you lee helm and causes the bow to fall off. The more it falls off, the farther out the main has to be backed to be effective. So the skipper has to get the feel of the boat and know just how much he or she must head up to counteract this tendency to fall off. The only way is to practice. If you don't learn to stop the boat in a hurry, you may find yourself going over the starting line too early, needlessly.

Last-Minute Wind Shifts

On light, fluky days a wind shift just before the start of a race can mean the difference between winning and losing. An observant crew can be very valuable in such instances. In one national championship I sailed, the buoy end was favored in very light breezes. We noticed some dark patches on the water approaching the Committee Boat end and immediately sailed over there. We reached the new breeze just as the starting gun sounded and won the race easily. One other lesson was learned: The crew of another boat also saw the dark patches of wind, but instead of just verbally describing the location of the breeze to his skipper, he pointed to it. I expected that the mistake would draw many boats from the rest of the fleet over to the new wind. Fortunately, however, only one other crew noticed the crewman point. The lesson learned about pointing was the third boat to notice the new wind got a second in the race, while the one with the pointing crewman lost a sure second place and wound up third. So never point at anything unless you are doing so to deliberately mislead your competitors.

Though the above is an extreme example, there are many times when a lesser wind shift can have a great effect on the start of a race. Later we will discuss the favored end of the line, which is the upwind end. A small wind shift can change one end of the line from being favored and make the other end favored. It's important to be aware of such shifts; they can account for many boat lengths when the race starts.

Potential Tactical Problems

The skipper and crew have to be constantly aware of the position of competitors before the start. They particularly have to keep another boat from getting an overlap to leeward and forcing them over the line early or closing any opening they might have at the Committee Boat. Often boats approach on port tack and tack into a leeward position onto starboard tack. The skipper and crew need to anticipate this, possibly by heading off and discouraging the port tack boat from tacking, though not obstructing it from keeping clear. If she tacks anyway, then head back up again to increase the lateral distance between the two boats. A crew member can be calling to the skipper the likelihood of port tack boats attempting this maneuver. He should also advise the skipper whether it looks as if they are "running out of line." In other words, are they going to reach the end of the line before the gun goes off. If that happens they have only two choices, neither good: (1) go over the line early in which case they must return to restart, or (2) go under (to leeward) of the starting mark, which, though more desirable, can't be done if a boat is to leeward of them holding them up. They could avoid running out of line by controlling their progress along the line by judicious luffing and speed control.

Over Early

The last duty previously mentioned was being aware of whether the Race Committee was calling you back for being over the line early. Sometimes it's hard to judge if your bow or other part of the boat was over before the gun. Race Committees have different ways of informing you. Sometimes a board is held up with your sail number on it. Sometimes it's a gun or horn for each boat over early and the number called out on a megaphone. On cruising boat starts in major races, the premature starters are often announced on a certain frequency on the VHF radio. Whatever method is used will be written in the racing instructions passed out to the competitors before the race. However, it's the obligation of each boat to sail the course properly. Not being aware of the Race Committee's recall signal is no excuse. So it's very important, if it's a close start, for the skipper to know whether the boat is over early, and one of the crew should be assigned the task of watching the Race Committee for the recall. It has happened many times that a skipper has raced the entire race, crossed the finish line first, and not received the traditional gun for first place, only to learn he was a premature starter and technically hadn't raced the course properly.

Those are the various duties of the crew. Following are input considerations that are primarily the concern of the skipper.

INPUT CONSIDERATIONS FOR THE SKIPPER

Wind Direction

Finding wind direction is fairly easy. Just shoot the boat dead into the wind and let the sails luff. When the main and jib are right over centerline of the boat, you are headed directly into the wind. Wait until the boat has lost all headway while doing this (particularly in light airs) because if it is moving forward, the wind will appear to be dead ahead long before it really is. If there is a sea that is slightly angled to the wind direction, the jib is a better indicator than the main because the weight of the main boom tends to make it swing more. When you are dead into the wind, read the compass to get its direction.

Wind Type

You want to know, though it often ends up as an educated guess, whether the wind will be shifting back and forth (oscillating) or gradually veering or backing in one direction (a continual shift). Oscillating shifts are usually associated with unstable conditions. Upper air, for example, may be coming down to the surface in gusts as the air above the land rises.

Look at smoke coming from chimneys ashore. If it's a clear day with cumulus clouds, and if the wind is cool and from the northwest, you can be fairly sure the mean direction of the wind will remain fairly consistent, but the wind itself may shift back and forth in oscillating shifts. If it's a hazy day, the smoke from the stacks may go up a short way and then stratify along with the stratified clouds. If the wind has a southerly trend, the weather will be stable and the mean direction of the wind will probably shift one way or the other in a continual shift.

Another way to check out shifts before the start is to sail close-hauled on the port or starboard tack for a while and record the high and low compass headings on both tacks. If you do this, you'll know right after the start whether you are sailing in a header or a lift.

STARTING TACTICS

Favored End

Once you have determined the wind direction and decided what type it is, find out which end of the line is favored. It will be the end that is more upwind.

First, let's straighten out a few terms. Normally boats cross the starting line on starboard tack. The port end of the line, therefore, is called the leeward end because it's to leeward of the starboard tack boats. We often leave marks to port in the United States so the buoy is normally placed at the port end of the starting line. The Race Committee boat is at the starboard end.

You might think the upwind end should be called the "windward" end of the line, and some people do call it that. But this gets confusing when the buoy end, or the leeward end, is upwind. It is preferable to call the upwind end the "favored" end of the starting line.

If the first leg is a beat, we want to know which end is more upwind. The position of the first mark has nothing to do with the end of the starting line you choose. For instance, the first mark could be so far over to the right side of the course that you could practically lay it on port tack. The natural assumption would be that the starboard end is closer, and it is by straight-line distance. But if no boat on the line can lay the weather mark (sail to it on one tack from the start) and the port end is more upwind, the port end is favored.

Look at Figure 6-2. If the wind is square, or perpendicular to the starting line, a boat on the port tack starting at the buoy end will meet a boat starting at the other end on the starboard tack. The position of boats starting on a square line is indicated by the dashed line. It doesn't matter if they start on opposite tacks or start on the same tack and meet later going up the weather leg. Assuming equal speed and no wind shifts, the effect will be the same.

Now, shift the wind 10° to the left. The new position of the two boats when they meet is indicated by the dotted line. The boat that started at the

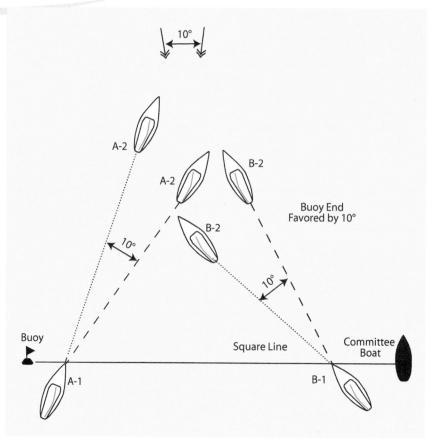

Figure 6-2. When the wind shifts 10° to the left, the buoy end is favored and boat A will be ahead of boat B.

port end of the line now is able to cross the boat that started at the Committee Boat end. As long as there is at least one tack on the weather leg that will make their paths cross, Boat A will have an advantage over Boat B.

There are a number of ways to determine the favored end. Possibly the most popular is shooting head to wind in the middle of the starting line. The upwind end will be forward of abeam. A more accurate way of doing the same thing is to shoot the wind just outside the buoy end and sight in one direction, toward the Committee Boat. This halves any potential error. If the Committee Boat is abaft abeam (as shown in Figure 6-3), the buoy end is favored.

Most boats have a thwart or a traveler that runs directly across the boat, and this can facilitate sighting. If these aren't available, lines painted on the deck perpendicular to the centerline will do the same thing. Note that in Figure 6-3 Boat A shoots the wind in the middle of the line, sights abeam, and concludes that the buoy end seems to be favored. But when Boat B shoots into the wind near the buoy, it is obvious which end is.

The recommended length of a starting line in heavy air is 125% of the aggregate length of all the boats crossing it. For example, if you had twenty 30-foot sailboats on a line, it should be 750 feet long. If the wind is 5° off a perfect 90° angle, a boat starting at the upwind end will be 65.6 feet ahead of a boat at the other end, right at the start! This is over two boat lengths!

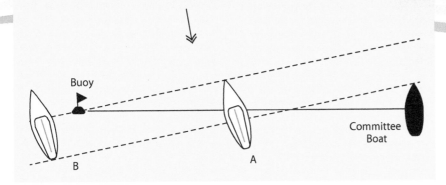

Figure 6-3. Shooting head to the wind before the start can help determine the favored end. Here the buoy end is favored.

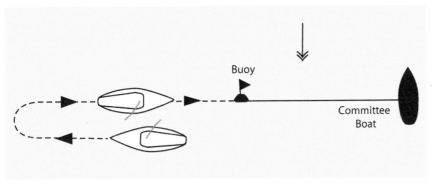

Figure 6-4. Checking wind direction on a compass when sailing a range along the line is another method for determining the favored end.

Imagine the penalty you would pay if you started at the wrong end if the wind were 15° off square.

If you have a boat with a steady compass, an accurate method is to compare the compass course of the starting line with the compass reading of wind direction. Sail away from the buoy end of the starting line. Then sail back toward it on the extension of the line, lining up the buoy with the white flag on the Committee Boat. When you are sailing that range, check the compass heading. (See Figure 6-4.)

Let's say you find the line to be 100° as you sail toward the Committee Boat. That means the wind direction should be 010° (100° minus 90°) if the wind were absolutely square to the line and neither end was favored. Then remember this "magic number" of 010° every time you shoot the wind thereafter.

Check the wind direction quite often to make sure there hasn't been a shift in the interim. If you find the wind is 15°, then the Committee Boat end is now favored by 5°. There is one major advantage to this system—you don't have to be near or on the starting line every time you check the wind.

Quite often there are other classes that may start ahead of you and you won't be allowed near the line until a few minutes before you start. This is usually too late to get all the other input considerations. There's normally just enough time to get where you want to be, and then make one last wind check to be sure nothing has changed.

Another reason to check wind direction away from the line is that the wind can be "chewed up" by the many boats sailing around at the start. Getting an accurate wind direction there may be very difficult.

Running the Line

There are very few fixed points in the water you can use as reference with which to judge distance. There are, however, two fixed points you can use, and those are the buoy end of the line and the Committee Boat. By sailing the length of a starting line and timing it, you can get a good feel for time and distance as you approach the line to start. If the line is long, there's another good reason to time it. You may make a last-minute decision to start at the other end of the line. You had better know how long it will take for you to get there.

Current

Nothing is more frustrating or disastrous than misjudging the current and being swept across the starting line early, before the starting gun. It's particularly bad when it happens in a light breeze and you have to fight your-way back up current on a run. Equally bad is being caught far away from the line with the current against you when the wind dies. So the trick is to determine the current's speed and direction.

Observation is the key word. Observe how the Committee Boat or other boats lie at anchor. Look at the mark end and see if it leaves a wake (as if it were moving through the water). Look at small objects, preferably below the surface, that may float past the mark. Or even better, toss a current stick (a 2- to 3-foot stick weighted to remain upright with a few inches of it breaking the surface) overboard near the mark and observe its speed and direction of drift.

Course to the Windward Mark

Most skippers shoot the boat into the wind to determine wind direction, but not enough skippers point the boat in the direction of the first mark before the start. This can be useful information to have. If the course is a windward-leeward one, pointing your boat at the windward mark will tell you which side to set your spinnaker on—which tack you'll be on as you return on the run. When you point the boat at the mark, the sails will be luffing. If the mainsail is off-center and more to the port side of the boat, it means the wind direction is more from the right side of the course and the starboard tack will be the long tack up. If the starboard tack is the long tack when beating, you will be on the port tack on the run. (See Figure 6-5.) Of course, you must watch for further wind shifts as you beat up to the weather mark, which may change this information.

It's a racing axiom that, if all else is equal, it is best to take the long tack first since it takes you closer to the windward mark. Figure 6-5 also shows that by pointing your boat at the windward mark you can easily determine which is the long tack.

Another racing axiom is shown in Figure 6-6— take the upcurrent tack first. In the diagram the wind is square, but the current is off to the right. On the starboard tack, across the current, the boat is being

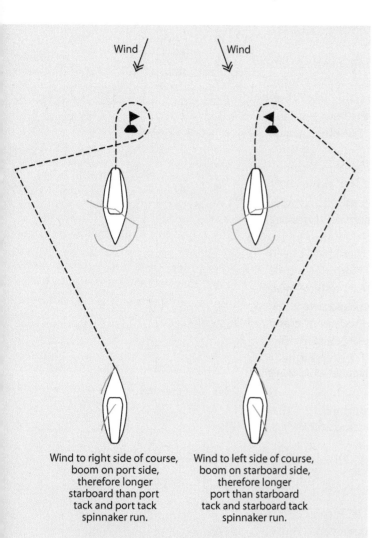

Wind to right side of course, boom on port side, therefore longer starboard than port tack and port tack spinnaker run.

Wind to left side of course, boom on starboard side, therefore longer port than starboard tack and starboard tack spinnaker run.

Figure 6-5. Sometime before the start, point your boat at the windward mark so that you can determine which tack to the mark will be the longest.

set away from the windward mark. This is effectively making the port tack the "long" tack and should be taken first (all else being equal).

Now we have covered the duties and input considerations necessary to enable the skipper to make reasonable starting decisions—let's look at the actual start.

Where to Start

At some point a decision must be made exactly where along the line you want to start. The choice is based on which end of the line is favored, and how the wind is expected to shift immediately after the start. For instance, the buoy end may be favored because the wind has shifted to the left momentarily. That means right after the start you'd be sailing in a starboard tack header and would want to tack away.

In this situation you might try starting a short distance from the buoy end in hopes you won't be pinned by other starboard tack boats when you want to tack over to port. If, however, you don't expect the wind to swing back to the right, but rather to swing farther to the left due to either meteorological or geographical reasons, the best start would be right at the buoy.

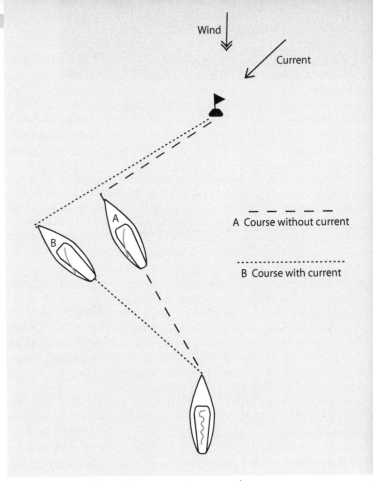

Figure 6-6. The effect of current on the approach to a windward mark. Boat B, being set by current, should have tacked early in the leg.

If the Committee Boat end is favored or you expect the wind to swing to the right, that's the end to start at. In this case you would have to be careful not to be squeezed out by leeward boats. If the wind is steady and you want to remain on starboard tack, you had better be one of the first boats to cross the starting line, but you don't have to be right next to the Committee Boat.

You want good speed and room to fall off to leeward to increase your speed, or you may end up in the bad air (airflow that has been disturbed) of some other boat and have to tack away to get clear air. On the other hand, when you expect the wind to shift to the right, you must be next to the Committee Boat, so you can tack right after the start. You want to be sure no boat can get on your weather quarter and keep you from tacking from starboard.

The Starting Approach

When you trim in the sails just before the start, you won't be able to gain much speed unless you can bear off slightly. Just trimming in the sails when you are heading on a close-hauled course will cause the boat to make a great deal of leeway until it picks up sufficient speed to create adequate lift on the keel and rudder. It's impossible to bear off to pick up speed if there's a leeward boat right there, so avoid getting yourself into this predicament.

If you see a boat attempting to get its bow to leeward of your stern, discourage him unless the gun is just about to go. Try to open up a hole to leeward of you by luffing up boats to windward. At the last moment you can reach off into this hole and pick up speed.

Another reason to avoid letting a boat get close to leeward of you is more serious. He can force you right over the line before the gun and, if any part of your boat, equipment or crew is still there when the starting signal goes, you will have to restart.

SPECIAL STARTS

The Dip Start

This start is used quite often when there is a strong current running with the wind or a large sag in the middle of the starting line. It consists of dipping across the line from the course side and starting. It's dangerous on two counts. First, you are on the wrong side of the line and have to get completely over to the other side of the line before the starting gun goes. If any part of your boat or crew is on the line when the gun goes, you are considered being over the line early (OCS—On Course Side) and have to restart. Along with this problem is the fact that you are not hidden from view from the Committee Boat as are many of the other boats that are approaching on starboard tack. You stick out like a sore thumb, and even if you get completely over to the proper side of the line before the gun goes, you may be called over early by an overzealous Race Committee member. The second problem is that, being weather boat, you have no "rights" (right-of-way) over leeward boats approaching the line on the same tack. They can hold you up and keep you on the wrong side of the line if they want to. The time that this type of start is advantageous is shown in Figure 6-7: when a light wind combines with a strong current in the same direction. Boat A stays on the upcurrent side of the line. This is good practice in

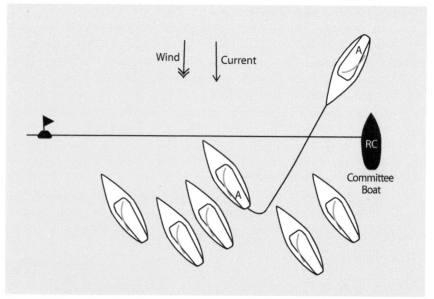

Figure 6-7. Boat A makes a dip start, useful when light air and strong current come from the same direction.

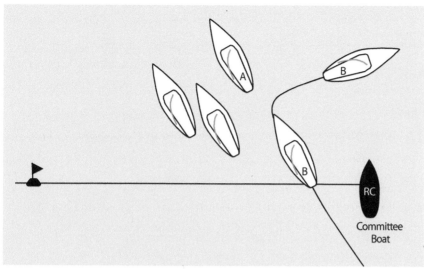

Figure 6-8. Boat B makes a delayed start and tacks away for clear air.

light air since, if the breeze dies, the current can carry you far downwind of the starting line. It may take a very long time to get back. Just before the gun Boat A dips over the line to the proper side and starts. Often the other boats haven't allowed for the current and are late for the start. This opens a hole for Boat A to dip into.

There is one time you cannot do a dip start. After a general recall (a start when the whole fleet is recalled, because so many boats are over early the Committee can't tell which specific boats were over), a boat on the wrong side of the line in the last minute before the starting signal has to go around either end of the line to start. This is called the "One Minute Rule."

The Delayed Start

If the Committee Boat end of the starting line is well favored, many boats will decide to start there. It's very important to be able to tack away and clear your air if there are boats on top of you. If there's a jam-up at the Committee Boat, this may be very difficult to do. You can't tack on to port if there are starboard tack boats to windward and behind you. You have to wait until they tack away first. One solution, if you see a jam-up developing before the start, is to be in the second wave, but be right next to the Committee Boat. As you cross the line, therefore, there is no way for a boat to be to windward of you and prevent you from tacking to port to clear your air. This is accepting second best since the best start is made by the one boat that is closest to the Committee Boat at the gun, but the delayed start is far better than being buried in a pile of boats and pinned down. In Figure 6-8, Boat B has made a delayed start right behind boat A.

The Port Tack Approach

This is a start that takes guts. The whole fleet may be approaching the line on starboard tack with right-of-way, and you are converging with them on port tack "across the grain." Previously, they had to hold their course under

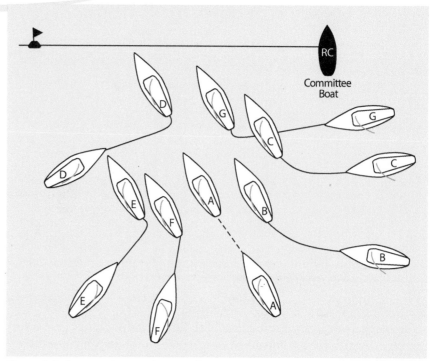

Figure 6-9. A port tack start takes guts, but Boat D finds a hole to tack into and gets a good start.

the rules so as not to obstruct you in your efforts to keep clear of them. However, under the new rules, after the gun the starboard tack boats can assume their proper course. This means, if they were reaching along the line, they can come up to close-hauled when the gun goes, and if you're in the way on port tack, that's just too bad. The advantage of a port tack approach is you can look for an open area in the fleet of starboard tack boats and tack into it if you find one. Once on starboard, you are pretty well committed to the same general area in the fleet. If you get on starboard early, you will find boats tacking in front of you, to leeward of you, and swooping down from the windward side. You can find yourself virtually boxed in by other boats and unable to get away from their "dirty" (disturbed, turbulent) air.

In Figure 6-9, Boat A approached the starting line closehauled on starboard tack from quite a long way out. Boats B, C, E, F, and G, in delaying their final approach, have completely surrounded her. Boat D has made a port tack approach, found a good hole, and is in a fine position to bear off for speed to make a good start.

Port Tack Starts

A port tack start can be successful when the buoy end is so favored that the boats on starboard tack can barely cross the starting line. They end up in one long line, bow to the stern of the boat ahead. If a port tacker can cross the lead starboard tack boat, he or she crosses them all. A current in the same direction as the wind enhances the chance of success.

The joy of a risky port tack start is when you cross the lead boat you cross the fleet, are in first place, and have clear air with nobody near you.

Light-Air Starts

The most crucial thing in a light-air start is to stay near the starting line. Though you should always stay near the line, it's particularly important in light air. I've seen boats that under normal wind conditions would be no more than thirty seconds from the line take an hour to cross the line, while the rest of the fleet is sailing merrily up the windward leg in a local breeze. Second, always have the anchor ready to put over the side if the breeze dies completely, particularly if a current is carrying you away from the line.

It has been interpreted as perfectly legal to have the anchor sit on the course side of the line as long as the boat itself is on the proper side when the gun goes. However, it is illegal to pull the boat forward with the anchor when you raise the anchor.

For light-air starts, keep your speed up, because it's very difficult to get moving again if you luff your sails and kill your speed. Also, don't rely on a timed start, because the breeze may be fresher as you go away from the line than when you return.

When you make any maneuver, a tack or a jibe, in current and light air, keep in mind what effect the current will have on your relationship to the starting line after the maneuver is completed. It is usually best to choose between tacking or jibing based upon which heads you into the current. For instance, if the current is carrying you downwind away from the line and you jibe to come back toward the line, by the time you complete your jibe you will be much farther away from the line than before. However, if you tack, you will most likely be almost the same distance away from the line at the end of the tack as you were when you started the tack.

TEST QUESTIONS

1. Which comes first, the warning signal or the preparatory signal?
2. Which represents the true starting sequence time, the gun or the shape?
3. What is a Vanderbilt start?
4. What is an "oscillating shift"?
5. How do you determine the "favored" end of the starting line?
6. What does pointing the boat at the windward mark tell you?
7. What is a "current stick"?
8. What is a "dip start"?
9. Why would you do a "delayed start"?
10. What benefits are there in a port tack start?

Racing Tactics

CLEAR AIR

Once the starting gun or horn has gone off, getting and keeping clear air becomes of prime importance. Wind in the proximity of a starting line always is chopped up by the boats, so those that get away from the start area into clear air first will be able to stretch their lead. If you find yourself boxed between boats to windward and leeward of you, get out of there! This may mean killing your speed, if necessary, so that you can let the windward boat pass. You can then cross under its stern when you tack.

Clear air is important anywhere on the course, but particularly so near the start. Figure 7-1 shows the various zones of disturbed air coming from a sailboat. The shadings indicate the intensity of the effect. The darker the area, the more detrimental it is for you to be there.

The distance the disturbed air extends to leeward and astern will depend on the wind conditions. As a general rule, air is disturbed at a greater distance in light air than it is in heavy. You probably would be affected adversely by a boat two to four lengths to windward of you in heavy air. But it can run up to seven lengths in light air.

The worst area is the blanket zone where a boat is ahead and upwind of you. Most of the diagrams I've seen show this zone as a cone flowing straight to leeward of the windward boat's sails, and though this is technically correct, I prefer to show it as a curve. For some reason, possibly having to do with the fact that the apparent wind is farther aft at the top of the mast than at the bottom, a curve seems to better depict what actually happens on the boat. This will become apparent if you've ever been on a large cruising boat on a beam reach and have passed to windward of a small boat. Your bow must be well past his before you cause him to straighten up.

If you're racing a class boat and are trying to hurt a competitor on a reach, you'll find it insufficient to have your masthead fly pointing at his mast.

You will probably have to get well past him, so that your fly points ahead of his bow before you begin

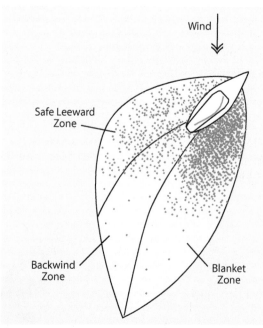

Figure 7-1. Competitors sailing in any of the shaded areas would be sailing in the leading boat's "bad air."

to have any effect on him. Once you do get a boat in your blanket zone, however, he will drop back quickly.

When close-hauled, a boat astern and slightly to leeward will be in the backwind zone. Though this is a bad position to be in, it's not as harmful as being blanketed and you won't drop back as fast. Still, the turbulent airflow you are receiving from the other boat's sails is usually sufficient to necessitate a tack to clear your air.

Just to windward of the backwind zone is what is called the safe leeward zone. A boat sailing this area generally will not be able to pass to windward of the leading boat. The lead boat has what is called a "safe leeward position." As the wind hits the sails of the lead boat, it will be bent aft. This means the boat to windward and behind will be sailing in an apparent header. The wind will be more on the bow than it is for the lead boat. In this situation, the boat is affected more by a change in wind direction than it is by turbulence. The leeward boat can affect the windward boat on its quarter by pinching. If that doesn't work, bring your traveler to windward of the centerline. The turbulent airflow off your mainsail will be directed upwind and have an immediate detrimental effect on the windward boat. They will drop back incredibly fast. Try it. It works. An aggressive sailor will try to slow other boats in a race by keeping all these zones in mind and using them properly.

COVERING

Because there are many potential winners in a race and you can't slow them all, you should only cover those who might provide a serious threat to your own position. The basic rule in all covering situations is "stay between your competition and the mark."

If you are headed for the windward mark and you tack hard on the wind of a competitor, placing it in your blanket zone, it will be forced to tack away. To cover, you will have to tack as well. This is called a close cover and should be used only when you want a competitor to tack. A loose cover is one where you allow your competitor to have free air so that he won't be inclined to tack away.

The close cover is used when a rival is sailing away from the desired side of the course or away from a group of boats you should cover. Here it is important to force him to tack. In effect, you shepherd him back in the desired direction. A loose cover can be used when the rival boat is on the tack on which you want to remain.

BREAKING COVER

Breaking a close cover depends a great deal on the exact positions of the boats. Let's assume you are sailing bow to bow on port tack with a boat just to weather of you. You are both approaching the layline. Your competitor has you pinned, and every time you bear off to try and get tacking room, he or she bears off too.

As leeward boat you can sharply push him head to wind. But make sure you ease your jib so that it doesn't back you over onto the other tack (particularly important with a genoa). You may very well catch him enough by surprise that he will fail to ease his jib in time. The result will be that he will fall off on the other tack short of the layline. You can now go on until you reach the layline and starboard tack him near the mark when you come together again (assuming marks are rounded to port).

However, a luff may be impossible because you are well to leeward and behind. Here, a series of tacks may just discourage the coverer, especially if he feels he is losing ground to other boats by engaging in this private tacking duel. If he is not discouraged, which would be the case if you are the only boat that poses an immediate threat, or if it's a match race series, a "false" tack can sometimes work. This tack appears exactly like a tack up to the head-to-wind point, but then you fall back on the original tack.

Your crew must know the tack will be a false one, but must make it appear to be authentic by freeing the jib, crossing the boat, and doing whatever else is normally done on the boat during a tack. Hopefully, the overanxious coverer will tack too quickly, and after completing his tack, will have to regain speed in order to tack back again.

A false tack rarely works when the covering boat is looking for it and is prepared to delay its tack until your intentions are obvious. In that case you had better complete your own tack, because any hesitation when head-to-wind will lose you ground. Theatrical acting, along with a louder than usual "ready about," rarely works either, although some sailors try it.

If you are still unable to shake clear of the covering boat and you are approaching the layline, to leeward and behind the covering boat, your only hope is that he will overstand. If he is so intent on covering you, he may not notice that he's on the layline. The proper thing to do is to keep on going. Don't tack until he tacks. Pinch your boat to get as far to windward as possible. This will slow you down, and your coverer may become gleeful at how badly he's "hurting" you and how much he's pulling ahead.

Actually, the farther he goes, the greater the distance he sails away from the mark. Figure 7-2 shows Boat B pinching with Boat A footing out. At position 1, A is closer to the mark and, because A is on the layline, she will obviously beat B to the mark. At position 2, however, B is closer to the mark (the dotted radius lines), and when they tack, B will have at least an inside overlap at the mark, which basically means that she has taken over the lead. B may even be totally clear ahead of A, and though it is possible for A to override B if they are planing boats, getting A to overstand is the only chance B has to get ahead in this situation.

Opportunities for breaking cover sometimes will appear as a problem on the covering boat. You may round a leeward mark behind and want to tack, but you know that if you do, you will be covered by the lead boat. Wait until their crew is engrossed in some problem or action and then tack. If crew members on the other boat are up on the foredeck getting the spin-

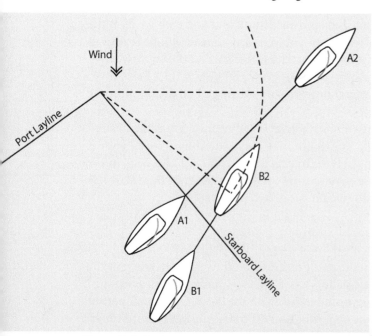

Figure 7-2. Getting a competitor to overstand the mark, as B2 does to A2 in this drawing, is sometimes the only chance to get ahead.

naker pole down, that is the time to tack away. Always try to tack when their attention is focused on something else.

Another way to break a cover is to get a third boat to run interference. If you are on port tack and being covered, you may see another boat, possibly in another class up ahead. Time your tack so that if the covering boat tacks when you do, it will be sailing right up the backwind of the disinterested third boat. When the skipper realizes the mistake, he or she will have to tack away and you'll have broken the cover.

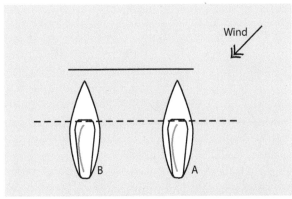

Figure 7-3. Boats A and B are side-by-side and appear to be even.

Wind Shifts

More can be gained or lost in one healthy wind shift than can usually be made up by any amount of boat speed or superior sailing. But a beginning racing skipper often is so concerned about whether his or her boat is sailing faster than the one next to him, he neglects to consider the effect of a wind shift. He fails to recognize wind shifts when they arrive and doesn't know how to handle them properly.

Discussing any wind shift with a skipper who can't steer within 10° of a close-hauled course (because he's too worried about other boats) is useless. Half the time, he's luffing and can't determine the shift even if it is 20°! So a basic premise is that you must at least be able to sail the boat well enough to know that a luff indicates a wind shift, and not erratic steering.

How do we determine a shift? Many people use landmarks, but this is only good for short runs, in fact only for one tack. Once a boat has been tacked twice, the angle to the landmark is different and is no longer reliable.

For boats with compasses, a crew member should be continuously calling the compass reading to the skipper. But after hearing a long string of compass readings, a skipper can get confused about just which way the wind has shifted. As a memory aid, make two assumptions: (1) that a boat on starboard tack is superior to a boat on port tack, and (2) that a lift is good and a header bad. It then follows that on starboard tack, the higher numbers are good, on port tack the higher numbers are bad. This may be a little oblique but it can tend to eliminate confusion. Thus, if you are sailing 275° on starboard tack and a short time later the crew calls out 280°, you have been lifted. On port tack you have, of course, taken a header.

A third way to determine wind shifts is by your relative position to other boats. This is used most often on small boats, like Finn dinghies, that either don't carry compasses or are bouncing around too much for them to be dependable. Of course, the skipper of a singlehanded boat doesn't have a crew to read compass headings to him.

In Figure 7-3, the two boats A and B are abeam of each other. In Figure 7-4, the wind has headed the boats and B has "shot" ahead, even though the distance from each other hasn't changed (note the dashed line through the mast). In Figure 7-5, both have been lifted and A appears to be ahead of B.

If you're sailing B in Figure 7-4, it's quite easy to attribute the sudden

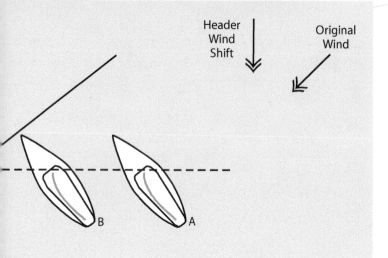

Figure 7-4. In a header Boat B appears to be ahead.

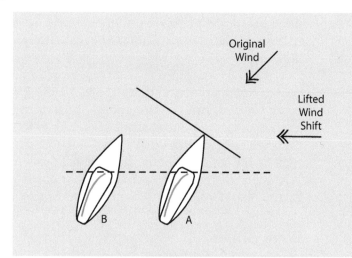

Figure 7-5. In a lift Boat A appears to be ahead.

lead to superior helmsmanship, some extra little trim on the mainsheet, or a minor adjustment to the traveler. In fact, anything that suits the ego will do—except the real reason—that you've both been headed and you ought to tack.

Why should you tack in a header? The classic description of why one tacks in headers can be shown by exaggeration. Imagine a north wind that's shifting back and forth from NE to NW. The boat in Figure 7-6 tacks on headers and is on port tack in the NW wind (1). When the wind heads him (2), he tacks to starboard and is on starboard tack in the NE wind (3). Boat B in Figure 7-7 tacks on lifts. He is on starboard tack in the NW wind (1) and port in the NE wind (2). You can see that the boat that tacks in headers is sailing straight up the course toward the windward mark while the other is sailing back and forth across the course. This never happens to such extremes, but the same occurs in small wind shifts with smaller gains and losses.

For this reason, given the choice between the two situations shown in Figures 7-4 and 7-5, many skippers elect to be on Boat A in Figure 7-5. Not only is he to windward of the other boat, but if a lift comes, he goes well ahead of B. This is called being on the inside of a lift. The only hitch is if the wind continues to shift in the same direction. (See Figure 7-8.)

Every time the skipper wants to tack to lay the windward mark, he gets lifted more and, as a result, cannot lay it. Most racing skippers call this "sailing the great circle route." Instead of gloating over how he is putting it to Boat B (see Figure 7-5), Boat A should be concerned that this may be a permanent shift to the right (see Figure 7-8). Perhaps he should tack when he gets farther lifted at point B.

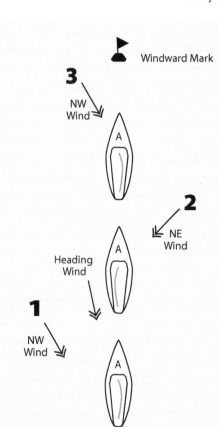

Figure 7-6. With a north wind that oscillates from NW to NE, Boat A tacks on headers and can sail a straight-line course toward the windward mark.

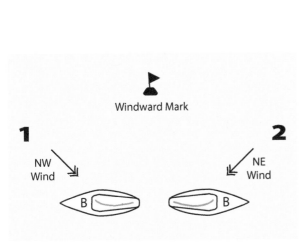

Figure 7-7. In the same oscillating wind, Boat B tacks on lifts and moves farther from the mark.

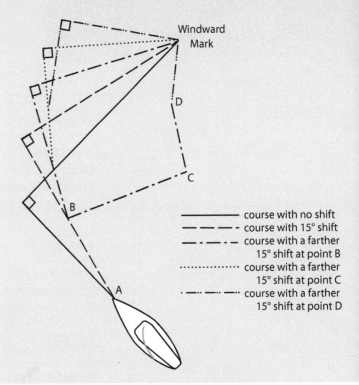

————————	course with no shift
– – – – – –	course with 15° shift
–·–·–·–·	course with a farther 15° shift at point B
··············	course with a farther 15° shift at point C
·– ··– ··– ··	course with a farther 15° shift at point D

Figure 7-8. Tack early if you expect a continual lifting wind shift.

If he had tacked at point B, taken his beating (sailing in a header), and tacked again at point C when he was farther headed, he would have come out far better in the long run.

It's this very problem that makes Boat B's position (in Figure 7-3) slightly superior. If lifted, he is more apt to tack away from A and get on the proper side of the shift. If headed, he is ahead of A, remains ahead after tacking, and increases his lead as the wind lifts him up to the mark.

The late Peter Barrett, Finn and Star Olympic gold medalist, was the first to describe another way of looking at the relationships of boats in a wind shift. He described boats as being even with each other upwind if they are all on a line perpendicular to the wind direction. He called them "lines of equal position." In Figure 7-9, Boats A, B, and C are all equally upwind. They are touching the solid line perpendicular to the wind direction. If either A or B tacked, they would meet C bow to bow. None is ahead of the others.

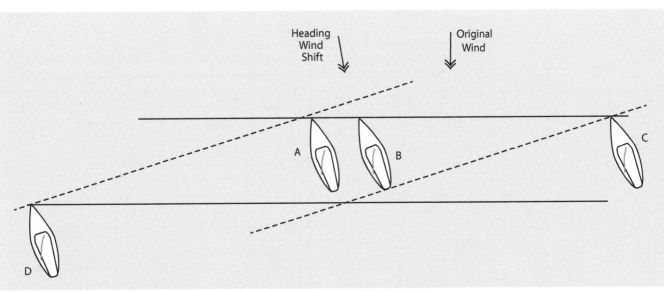

Figure 7-9. If you expect a header, sail to the side of the course you expect it to come from.

Boat D, however, is tail-end Charlie, well behind and to leeward. Along comes a heading wind shift (see dotted lines). If lines of equal position are drawn perpendicular to the new wind direction, we see that tail-end Charlie, Boat D, now leads the fleet with Boat A in second place, B third, and C running a poor last! This means that if you expect a header, for some meteorological or geographical reason, always sail to the side of the course it's expected to come from.

Laylines

Though a great deal of importance is always placed on getting a good start, getting around the first mark, which is often more congested than the start, is usually overlooked.

One universal comment made concerning the windward mark approach is "never get to the layline too early." The layline is the imaginary line on which a boat can reach a mark without having to tack again. Any boat that goes past this imaginary line has "overstood" the mark and will have to ease sheets and reach down for it. If you are a few hundred yards from the mark, it is practically impossible to judge accurately whether or not you can lay it. If you've gone too far, you have overstood and wasted distance. If you haven't gone far enough, you will have to tack twice again.

Even if you've judged the layline accurately, a wind shift can hurt you. In Figure 7-10, Boat A is on the layline and Boat B is the same linear distance away from the mark. But a header (W2) places the boats in positions A2 and B2. Boat B is now well ahead of A. Or a lift (W3) causes A to over-

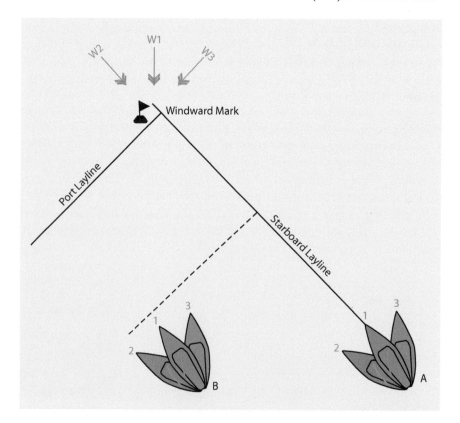

Figure 7-10. Avoid reaching the layline too early.

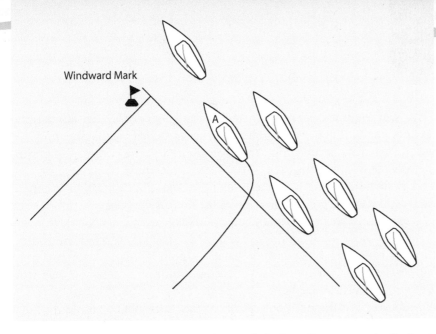

Windward Mark

A

Figure 7-11. Boat A heads to the layline on port and finds room to tack to starboard about three boat lengths from the mark.

stand the mark and have to reach for it while Boat B can practically lay it from a much shorter distance out.

Another disadvantage of getting to the layline early concerns the possibility that boats who are ahead of you will reach the layline and will tack in front of you, giving you bad air all the way to the mark.

The best approach is: Hit the starboard tack layline (for a port rounding) only four to ten boat lengths from the mark, depending on the size of the fleet. The larger the fleet, the farther out from the mark you have to be, because of congestion. Usually you can find a hole to tack into, for when boats tack on the layline, they tend to stack up to windward. Either they overstand or pinch up to avoid being directly behind another boat in his backwind.

If you are close to the mark, you probably can tack right behind one boat and on the lee bow of another (Figure 7-11). Even though you may have to duck under a few sterns to find a hole, generally you can gain many more boats than by getting to the layline early.

One disadvantage to this approach, even though it is a slight one, is the lack of time available on the starboard tack to prepare for a spinnaker set. This is usually not terribly important on a small boat, but as the boat gets larger, more time is needed to set up for the spinnaker.

The beginning racing sailor often makes the mistake of concentrating on the mark. I call it "mark fixation." As he or she approaches the mark, the novice will get on the layline quite a distance out. Then, because of current or wind shift, the layline changes. When this happens, the boat is either overstanding or not making the mark. But because the beginner is steering for the mark and not by the wind, he or she will either start bearing off without adjusting sheets or start pinching.

In a current, I've often seen skippers pinch more and more as they approach the mark until they're right next to it. But they are dead in the water and they drift into it. They don't realize what they are doing until the very end, and then they do not have enough way on to tack.

When you have tacked for the mark from a good distance out, ignore the mark until you get close. Have your crew tell you if you need to ease off or if you're not making it. Take two extra tacks if necessary, though you may be able to shoot head-to-wind at the last moment if you have good boat speed. Once you pinch though, you're dead.

"Tacking lines" are often painted on the decks of racing sailboats by their skippers. If you are approaching the starboard tack layline on port tack from a distance out, you can judge when the mark comes in line with the painted line. If a boat tacks in 90°, the line would be painted on the deck perpendicular to the centerline of the boat. If it can tack in less than 90°, the line would point more toward the bow of the boat.

Such lines are only a rough guide and only hold true if (1) the skipper is right on the wind when the sighting is taken, (2) there is no wind shift, (3) there is no current, and (4) the boat will point as high on one tack as it will on the other, which is a rare occurrence unless the seas and the wind are running exactly together.

As you pass the stern of a starboard tack boat, often you can see how far it is from laying the mark and can estimate how much farther you have to go. This can be done with accuracy only if you make your sighting just as its headstay and mast line up. Be aware that a foxy competitor may head down just at that moment to make you believe he or she is far from laying the mark and trick you into overstanding.

One of the worst mistakes, and one frequently made by racing sailors, is to be surprised by a starboard tack boat at or near the layline as it approaches it on port. You should always be looking for right-of-way boats when you are sailing on port tack, but particularly so near the layline.

If you are surprised by a "starboard" hail, and you have to do a panic tack over to starboard, the other boat will most likely ride right over you before you pick up speed. This will slow you enough for other boats on the layline to pass you.

It's also very possible you won't fetch the mark because of the leeway you will make from being slowed down by other boats. You must be aware of the starboard boat early enough to make the decision to either tack, if you feel it is laying the mark and you can get a safe leeward on it, or to go under its stern if it isn't laying. If you decide on the latter, then bear off early and substantially, easing both jib and main sheets as you do, and aim your bow at its stern. As it passes, you should be coming up and trimming in both the main and jib sheet for acceleration. The only time you might not pass this way would be if it's blowing like stink and you tend to be over-powered when you bear off. In that case, slowing the boat by luffing the sails slightly would probably be as satisfactory.

Often novice racers wonder why they can't luff up to kill their speed a little and then pass under a stern slightly more to windward. They feel that the more to windward you get the better it is. The answer is that one's position is being controlled by the starboard tack boat, and whether a port tack boat passes a foot farther to leeward, or a foot farther to windward, it is still a foot from the other fellow's stern.

If you do bear off, it is a good idea to yell: "Hold your course, I'm going under you." This has no basis in the rules, but he may not know this or may have to think about it. Legally, he can ignore the hail and tack right on you as long as he doesn't get involved in tacking too close. However, if you've headed well down to go under him and he tacks early, you might be able to go above him and pass to windward before he gets moving. Or, if he tacks just as you are coming up under his stern, you have a good chance at achieving a safe leeward position on him. Always keep in mind, as you approach a starboard tack boat, that when you reach the mark you will want to starboard tack him. You can't afford to be pinned down if you can't make the mark, so it's crucial to judge whether or not he is laying it.

Another mistake often made by a beginning racing sailor is to be so ecstatic by having starboard tack right-of-way over a port tack boat that the novice loudly yells "starboard" at any opportunity. There are times, especially when you are on the starboard tack layline, that such a hail is detrimental. The port tack boat, if it is close to crossing, will be feeding you bad air if it tacks. Because you already are on the layline, you can't tack away and make a gain. A better hail is "go across, you can make it." That way, the port tacker might not bother you when he does tack, and he might even overstand the mark!

Mark Roundings

What counts when rounding a mark is your position not at the time of rounding, but about one minute later. This means you must anticipate where the other boats are going to end up after they round the mark, and what effect they will have on you. Your own rounding must take their movements into account and minimize the impact they will have on you.

Though you can pretty much choose how you want to round a leeward mark, your options are more limited when rounding a windward mark. However, there are several alternatives. If you've overstood, you may want to reach down to the layline outside the "zone," the area three boat lengths of the boat nearest to the mark, in order to break any possible overlap you might have created while reaching.

Figure 7-12 (on following page, not to scale) shows Boat A with an inside overlap on Boat B. But the overlap is broken when the boats arrive at position A2 and B2, because Boat B now has hardened up for the mark.

If B had continued to head straight to the mark from the overstanding position, her angle would have kept A in an overlapped position.

Another situation occurs when B is near the port tack layline and has A behind and to windward. (See Figure 7-13, page 83.) When B reaches the zone (three full lengths of the boat nearer the mark), A is not overlapped and not entitled to room. Only the basic port-starboard, windward-leeward, and tacking too close rules apply. So, though A can't demand room, she can keep B from tacking around the mark until she tacks (if A merely sails straight ahead).

B does have one recourse. Because she isn't tacking until she is past head-to-wind, B simply luffs right up next to the buoy. A can't afford to luff because she will find herself on the wrong side of the mark, so she dips under B's stern. At that point, B completes her tack around the mark, and goes into the lead.

The situation can be slightly different. Boat A, when she approaches the zone, is slightly overlapping Boat B. A good tactic for B is to luff A sharply, provided, of course, she is the leeward boat with rights. This often can break the overlap by the time the zone is reached.

Remember that if two boats on a beat are approaching the mark on

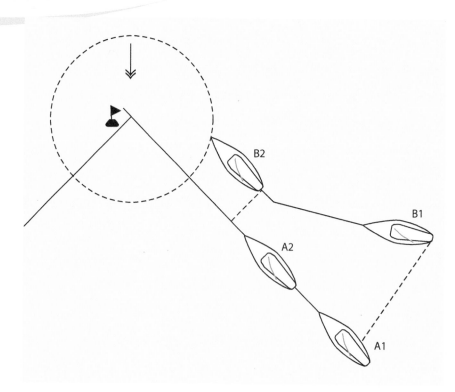

Figure 7-12. Boat B breaks an overlap by hardening up as it approaches the mark.

opposite tacks, the rules that apply stand as though the mark wasn't there. Don't, for example, tack right between a starboard tack boat and the mark, and claim room while luffing, unless you can get completely over to a close-hauled course on starboard and then luff up to get around the mark.

You have to complete your tack before you gain rights as a leeward boat, and you never have a right to room if the other boat is unable to give it. If you tack and luff too quickly for the other boat to respond, and you hit the mark because of it, that is your tough luck.

As you round a windward mark and head off on a reach, a lot depends on whether you have strong competition right on your heels, but a sharp luff from you is apt to discourage a boat astern from trying to pass to windward. If you have to hold low for the next mark, the trailing boat may use a delayed spinnaker set—assuming of course you're racing sailboats with spinnakers.

No matter how efficient your own crew work is, setting a spinnaker will slow you up slightly. The trailing boat will set jib for a reach, hike out hard, and concentrate on boat speed in an attempt to get on your wind. Once it's there and hurting you, that crew can set their spinnaker at leisure and still control you. You can't luff beneficially because you have your spinnaker set and the other boat has none. Your defense is to anticipate its intentions and not set until it does.

The decision whether to go high or low on the first reach must be made at the time you round the mark. There are many factors. If you expect the wind to increase, you can go high early in the light air for better boat speed, and come down later in the leg when the wind is strong enough to maintain speed on a freer point of sail. If the wind is light, but the current is strong, it's mandatory to stay upcurrent in case the breeze drops out more.

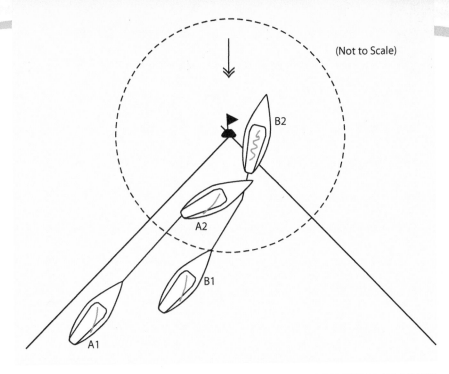

(Not to Scale)

Figure 7-13. Boat B takes the lead by luffing at the mark, forcing Boat A to dip her stern.

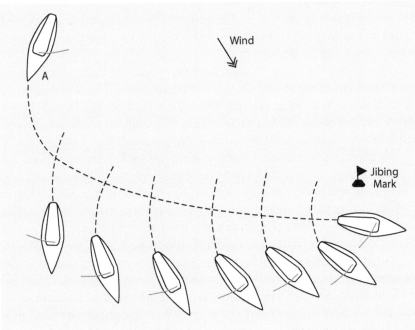

Wind

Jibing Mark

Figure 7-14. The outside boat (A) slows down and takes the stern of its competitors to get inside at the mark, and to windward of them all.

It is most important to think ahead to the next mark so that you are on the inside of your competitors and have buoy room on them.

If you do find yourself on the outside of a bunch of boats at the jibing mark, consider slowing the boat down, jibing early, and crossing their sterns to get inside and to windward on the next leg. (See Figure 7-14.)

To slow the boat on a reach, luff the sails, including collapsing the spinnaker, and head up. On a run, trim the main amidships and collapse the spinnaker. When close-hauled, head up, luff the main and jib, and push the main boom out against the wind. And in all cases, steer the boat through a series of sharp "s" turns.

By slowing up, the overlap is broken and an outside boat is able to jibe over and head for the mark. By the time it gets there, the group should be well past the mark. But even if they aren't, the inside boat will have been

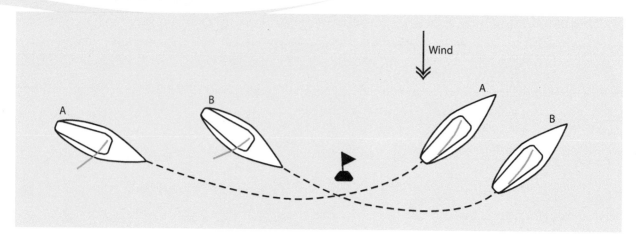

Wind

A   B   A   B

Figure 7-15. Boat A rounds up behind Boat B, cutting closer to the mark, and ends up to windward and ahead of B.

kept so close to the mark on the near side by the other boats that when she jibes, she will have rounded quite wide on the other side. This should allow the outside boat to sneak in.

Even if you aren't entitled to room, it's perfectly legal to take it if there's an opening available. A leeward boat can push you up into the mark though, so there's an element of risk.

Rounding the leeward mark is even more important. If you have a poor mark rounding there, you may never recover on the windward leg. Slowing down to break an overlap, then cutting in from the outside is very tricky, and the maneuver has to be started quite early or you will find yourself hard on the wind while you're trying to get inside.

If there is a tremendous jam-up at the leeward mark—it is often aggravated by light air and an adverse current—sometimes you can stay way wide of the mark and sail right around the fleet on the outside. Keep in mind if you are the inside or leading boat under these conditions, and leave your spinnaker set until the last possible moment.

If the wind is light and the current strong enough, you may want to sail right past the mark under spinnaker. I've seen boats that were just stemming the current under spinnaker, take it down a boat length from the mark, and take another five minutes to round the mark. In addition to the loss of drive from the spinnaker, the trailing boats caught up and took away what little wind was left.

Probably the most common error made by beginning racing sailors at a leeward mark rounding is to cut the mark too close on the near side. By the time the boat has rounded there's half to three-quarters of a boat length lost to windward, often much more if the sheets aren't trimmed in snappily.

This is room enough for a trailing boat, without buoy room rights, to cut inside. She is within her rights since the room is there to be taken. Any boat that rounds poorly will find a boat to weather controlling them and keeping them from tacking. If he is in the backwind zone of a boat ahead and can't tack away, the windward boat will probably drive through and he'll be even farther back.

The solution is to prepare for the rounding early with the spinnaker down, appropriate adjustments made for windward work, and the crew ready to trim in. When the bow is even with the mark, there should be close to a boat length of open water between it and the mark. As you trim around the mark, you should come onto a close-hauled course right next to it. If you are receiving room from outside boats, this can't be done, for they are only required to give you enough room to round safely, not to round in the fashion you've become accustomed to.

In Figure 7-15, Boat A is rounding the leeward mark the best way. She loses a little distance as she drifts out, but this is negligible compared to the distance lost to windward when she rounds like Boat B. If Boat B tries to end up where A is by making a sharper turn, her speed will be decreased because of it and she'll wind up making more leeway.

THE FINISH

The choice of which end of the finishing line to cross is the critical decision that consistently accounts for the most places won or lost in an upwind finish. Just as the upwind end of the line is favored at the start, the downwind end is favored at the finish.

In the 1968 Olympics, I saw Buddy Friedrichs, the U.S. skipper in the Dragon class, take four sterns and still finish first. Buddy was on port tack laying the starboard end, the Committee Boat end, of a long finish line. He met four other Dragons each on starboard tack one after another and ducked under the stern of each. Rather than tacking on him, they all continued toward the port (buoy) end of the line. By choosing the downwind end, Buddy went from fifth to first in a couple of hundred yards and won the gold medal.

As you approach the finish, you have four laylines to deal with: port and starboard laylines to the buoy end and the same to the Committee Boat end. The four laylines are shown in Figure 7-16 with the wind square to the line. You never want to sail past the first layline you reach if you can help it. When you reach the intersection of the laylines, you must make a judgment whether the Committee Boat or the buoy is closest and head toward the closest one—the one more downwind. Try to judge whether you are sailing more parallel to the finish line and, if so, take the other tack that crosses the line at a more acute angle.

If you know the ability of the race committee, you may be able to tell which end is favored simply by the wind direction. If the wind is straight down the course from the windward mark to the leeward mark, the finish line will be perpendicular to the course and neither end will be favored. If the wind has veered (clockwise) and the finish line is still perpendicular to the course line, the port end will be downwind. Race committees are expected to adjust slightly for the wind direction by splitting the distance between the finish line being square to the wind and being square to the course from the last mark. Thus it's a simple calculation that if the wind has shifted to the right, the left side of the line is downwind and vice versa. So keep the wind direction in mind during the last leg. If you are spending more time on the port tack than on the starboard tack, the wind has backed (shifted to the left) and the starboard end is downwind.

"Shooting" across the line is a useful tactic in trying to nip ahead of a close competitor. It works only in boats that carry a great deal of momentum, such as large displacement keelboats. It also works best on light days

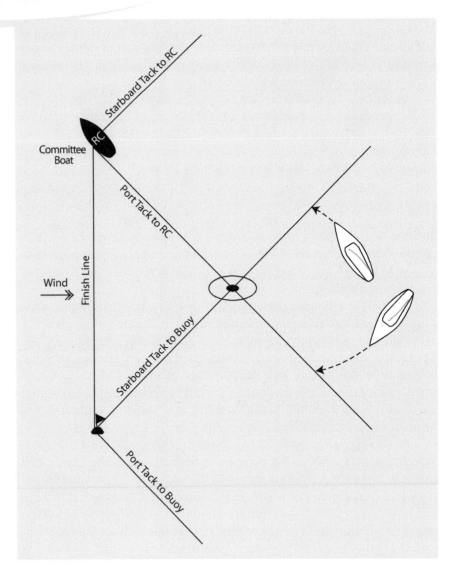

Wind

Committee
Boat

Finish Line

RC

Starboard Tack to RC

Port Tack to RC

Starboard Tack to Buoy

Port Tack to Buoy

Figure 7-16. Tack on the first layline to the finish that you reach.

rather than heavy. When the wind and seas are high, the boat is stopped quickly by the windage of the rigging and force of the seas against the bow. When you are about one boat length from the line, shoot dead into the wind. This cuts the sailing distance to the line substantially over another boat sailing at a 45° angle to the wind.

RACING RULES

There are numerous books out on racing rules, so it would be too much a duplication of effort to go into them deeply here. Instead we will touch on the most common ones. We've mentioned before that a starboard tack boat has right of way over a port tack boat, a leeward boat over a windward boat, and a yacht clear ahead over a yacht clear astern. A boat that catches up to the leeward side of a boat ahead cannot sail above her proper course, the "course a boat would sail to finish as soon as possible in the absence of the other boats referred to in the rule using the term." A leeward boat can luff a windward boat that is passing to keep it from getting ahead. However, it must initially give room to the windward boat and "must avoid contact if reasonably possible."

"Mark room" is "room for a boat to sail to the mark and then room to sail her proper course while at the mark." It does not apply to two boats approaching the windward mark on opposite tacks. Port-starboard applies, as does the "while tacking" rule that says "after a boat passes head to wind, she shall keep clear of other boats until she is on a close-hauled course."

As mentioned above, the "zone" is "the area around a mark within a distance of three hull lengths of the boat nearer to it. A boat is in the zone when any part of her hull is in the zone." If an inside boat has an overlap when the bow of the nearest boat reaches the zone, she is entitled to room to go around the mark. For a windward mark the boats would have to be on the same tack, but at a leeward mark it doesn't matter. It's a case where the port tack boat can have rights over a starboard tack boat.

If you hit a mark, you can exonerate yourself "after getting well clear of other boats as soon after the incident as possible" by taking a "one-turn penalty," a 360° turn that includes one tack and one jibe. In the past you were out of the race if you hit a mark.

If you go around a mark the wrong way, you can reround it so that a string representing your wake, when pulled tight, would look like the course of a boat that hadn't made the mistake.

When any part of your boat, equipment, or crew (in their normal position) crosses the finish line you are finished. You don't have to cross it completely, but can turn around and sail home if you'd like to. However, as long as any part of the boat is still on the finish line, you are still racing and subject to the rules. Thus, if you hit the mark or foul another boat you have to take the appropriate penalty.

Another boat cannot force you into an obstruction such as a moored boat or a shore just because they have right-of-way. You may request the chance to get out of the situation before damage is done by asking the other boat to tack away, allowing you to tack.

The rules are far more complicated than this short rundown indicates. As you race, your understanding of the rules will expand. You can also find a more experienced racer to explain them in more detail.

TEST QUESTIONS

1. What is a "safe leeward position"?
2. What is backwind?
3. Name one way of breaking cover.
4. What is a "loose" cover?
5. What are "lines of equal position"?
6. Why should you avoid laylines?
7. Why should you round a leeward mark very closely?
8. When is a boat tacking?
9. When can a leeward boat luff after starting?
10. I'm close-hauled on port tack approaching a windward mark. Can I demand buoy room from a starboard tack boat?
11. How does the "zone" affect buoy room rights?

Other Racing Tips

STEERING

Why is one skipper able to make a boat go faster than another? The key words are concentration and awareness. A good skipper concentrates not only on keeping the boat in the groove, but he or she also is aware of subtle changes in wind strength, wave direction, the relation of his/her boat to others, and a myriad of other speed and tactical factors. Relevant information can be transmitted to the skipper by his crew, but he or she is the one who has to sort it out, and do so without losing the ability to concentrate on steering.

The biggest problem a beginning racing sailor has comes from not paying adequate attention to steering. Steering is not an automatic thing, and when the beginner looks away at another boat or at the mark, orientation to the wind is lost. The result is that he or she may bear off or head up because his or her sense of awareness is not developed enough to feel that a change of course has caused a change to the boat's angle of heel.

A more experienced sailor will be aware of this change and will immediately correct for it. The best sailors will rely on their crews to feed them information about the location of other boats or marks so they won't have to look around at all.

Unfortunately, a novice racing sailor often gets a novice racing crew, since a better crew probably will want to be with a potential winner. This means the novice skipper usually has to gather all the information him- or herself until awareness does begin to develop.

The novice racing skipper must avoid oversteering. When sailing upwind there is a tendency to steer the boat first up and then down. As the boat heels over and develops some weather helm in a puff, the skipper should learn to let the tiller pull slightly to leeward. He or she must not push the tiller, though a novice often does.

When a boat is on a run, oversteering is most common among novices, and there are several reasons. First, there is no real feel to the boat since you have to steer in both directions. Second, the apparent wind direction shifts madly back and forth when sailing downwind. Third, the apparent wind speed is less than it is upwind, and it's more difficult to feel its direction. The wind is hitting the back of your head rather than blowing in your face. And finally, the seas tend to kick the boat's stern around.

A beginning racing skipper is likely to oversteer to avoid a downwind broach, but doing so may cause one. On a windy spinnaker run, he or she will be late in anticipating a wave, the wave gives the stern a shove, and he or she has to steer hard over to avoid a broach. Then the boat slews down the wave, and the helmsman has to steer hard the other way to avoid a jibe.

A fine practice exercise is what I call "non-steering." The next time you're on a windy spinnaker run and you're working madly to keep the boat on course, grit your teeth, tell yourself you're not going to steer, and simply hold the wheel amidships. It's amazing how the boat will settle down.

You may have to modify your resolve a little bit and compromise with half a turn of the wheel in either direction. But if you do this enough, you'll find yourself getting into the habit of steering only when it's necessary, and the result will be that your timing will improve greatly.

Remember, too, that any oversteering brakes the boat. You can test this by steering the boat through a series of sharp turns while on a light reach or run. You'll be amazed at how much the boat slows down.

One other mistake a novice racing sailor often makes on a one-design keelboat is to steer from the leeward side while beating. Though it is comfortable and easy to see the jib, you are unable to see and play the waves or see and allow for puffs. And your weight to leeward is detrimental even for a keelboat. Furthermore, when it's blowing hard, it's really not necessary to see the jib anyway, for most good sailors sail by the angle of heel. In short, though you may become good, you will never be a great sailor until you get used to steering from the windward side.

One final bit of advice on steering goes back to where we started: concentration. When some other boat is on your weather quarter and you want to tack, try forgetting about it and concentrate hard on steering. Recently, I found myself in that very situation in a pick-up Sunfish race. I was being run out to the layline by another boat to windward, and I kept looking back anxiously at him to see if I could cross him on port tack. After about a minute of maintaining the status quo, I said to myself, "This is ridiculous; if I can keep looking around at him and stay even, what can I do if I concentrate?" So I hiked out farther, played every wave and puff I could, and I knew without looking I'd soon be able to tack. When we did finally cross, the distance he was left behind in that short period of time was amazing!

CONCENTRATION EXPERIENCES

By "concentration" I mean to concentrate on the immediate job and/or goal and not be distracted by other influences. It's a pet peeve of mine to see skippers so distracted by a problem like a spinnaker twist that they forget to do their job of driving the boat as fast as possible through the water. One excellent example of the ability to concentrate came when I was crewing on a 5.5-meter sailboat for John Marshall, one of the principals of North Sails, the largest sailmaker in the world. It was before the start of a regatta and John decided that the jib we were flying was too flat, and we needed to change to a fuller and more powerful sail. The replacement jib was a zippered luff with a couple of teeth missing. The 5-minute signal had just gone, and John realized it was nip and tuck whether I could change the jib in time for the starting signal. I worked at it as fast as possible, the third crew member finally hauled up the new jib and trimmed it home just as the starting gun went and I jumped back into the cockpit. I looked up to see we had a perfect start at the favored buoy end of the line. John relied on me to do my job, and he, without distraction, concentrated on his job—to get the best start possible under the circumstances.

Here are a couple of more experiences that made me realize the importance of maintaining concentration. I was sailing in the 5.5-meter Olympic Trials in 1964 on Ernie Faye's boat *Pride*. We only had to win the last race to be the selected contender and sail in the Olympics in Japan. On the first weather leg, we were short of laying the weather mark, and the one boat we had to beat, Don McNamara's *Bingo,* crossed our stern on starboard tack and then tacked on port. We tacked on starboard, and as Don approached on port, he yelled "Hold your course, I'm going under you." Ernie didn't realize that since we had right-of-way, we could tack on top of Don as long as he didn't obstruct him. When we convinced Ernie to tack, we had lost the controlling position and Don had us beat on starboard tack at the mark. At this point Ernie lost his concentration, and it was difficult to get him to race the race on hand rather the race in the past. Anything can happen in sailboat racing and, in this case, it almost did. The corner of Don's jib pulled out on the final leg to the finish, so Don (a big guy) gave the helm to his crew and held the corner of the jib in position. We finished the race overlapped, *Bingo* going to Japan by half a boat length. I like the old Yogi Berra saying, "It ain't over 'till it's over." Experiences such as these make you realize that the race is never over until you cross the finish line.

In 1990, we were preparing for the Newport to Bermuda Race on a cat-ketch named *Denali*. Twenty-four hours before the start, long after the deadline for any changes to a competitor's rating, the race committee decided to penalize us by raising our rating. This meant we had to finish eight hours or so faster than under the previous rating to remain in the same finishing position. The owner was livid and so upset he could think of nothing else but this "injustice." I told him over and over again that "winning is the best revenge"—to get it behind him. Sure enough, we sailed over 200 miles to the west of the rhumb line, picked up a new breeze slant, and won the overall prize in the Bermuda Race. It's rare to win overall. I have raced Newport–Bermuda 20 times (even years only) and won only once. Concentrating on the project at hand and not on past problems or failures gives you the best chance of success.

PREPARATION

In the Gold Cup Regatta on International One Design sailboats in Bermuda, all competitors switched boats every day, so that no one would have a fast or a slow boat. It came down to the last race of the regatta to determine the winner between us and one other competitor. Before the start we sailed into a little secluded cove, and I went overboard with a towel to clean the bottom of the boat. I had learned years before in the '68 Olympic Trials how much a 2- to 3-day growth of slime on the bottom could slow a boat down. After the start, we sat on top of the boat we only had to keep out of first place to win the regatta. This means we stayed between the source of the wind and our competition. We disturbed his wind all the way up the first weather leg, until he was last and we were next to last. The fleet had halfway completed the next leg, so I suggested to Dr. Stuart Walker, our skipper, to break off and see how much we could catch up. We had blinding speed, and on the run, a usual equalizer for these boats, we were passing boats right and left. We finished the race in second or third place out of about 20 boats and won the regatta overall. A competitor at the prize party commented to me that they were copying everything we did on the run (crew weight position, spinnaker pole position, mainsail trim—very good "observation" on his part), but nothing worked. We still pulled away. "How did you do it?" he asked. Knowing we would be defending our championship the next year, I told him nothing. The tip is "Slime is slow."

LIGHT-AIR SAILING

All skippers and crews can look good in winds from 8 to 15 knots. It's heavy- and light-air conditions that really test you. Let's take a look at light-air conditions.

On light, "fluky," drifting days, you often hear how "lucky" some sailor was in a race because he or she got the wind first when it filled in. If you look at the record, though, you'll probably find that the same sailor is "lucky" most of the time. Probably he or she has a little more patience and concentration than the others, and has studied the weather and currents better. He or she may be more observant, noticing smoke, darkness on the water, or sails on other boats that might indicate a new breeze.

There are some things you can do to make your own boat sail faster in very light air. One of the most important techniques—discussed in Chapter 2 but worth repeating here—is to heel the boat slightly to leeward. At slow speeds, the friction of the water running past the hull is a greater drag factor than it is at higher speeds where wave-making drag becomes more important. Obviously, a clean, smooth bottom on the boat reduces friction.

Reducing the amount of hull surface in contact with the water (the wetted surface) also reduces friction. Heeling the boat lifts more hull surface out on the windward side than is submerged on the leeward side of most hull shapes. This net reduction in wetted surface reduces friction.

Heeling the boat has the added effect of allowing the sails to fall into their designed shape. For example, if three persons pick up a sail by the head, tack, and clew, it will take the shape designed in to it. But hang the sail vertically and it's a mess of wrinkles. Of course, when a puff does come, it will fill the sail, which then will start to pull for you. But if the boat already is heeled, the sail will start to pull immediately as the puff hits. And it will work with the slightest zephyr.

Another advantage to heeling the boat is the slight weather helm it will create. This gives lift to the rudder, helps reduce leeway, and makes it much easier for the helmsman to steer well.

To heel a boat, simply put the crew on the leeward side. This can be done in everything from dinghies to 12-meter boats. In other words, it's worth trying on any boat. Make sure the crew stays low and doesn't disturb the existing airflows. Remember, as stated in Chapter 2, that any crew movement in light air must be made very gently. Any thump or sudden movement can kill any forward momentum the boat has built up. Sails must be adjusted extremely slowly and carefully. A yank on the jib sheet can separate the airflow over the lee side of the sail, and it will take a second or two for it to attach itself again. On a small boat the winch handle often is used more in light air than in heavy to trim the jib just a click or two. Both the jib and main sheets must be constantly adjusted in light air, because the skipper can't turn the boat fast enough to follow the changes in wind direction. And if he or she did try to follow them, it would kill the speed.

In heavy air the reverse is usually the case. The sheets remain trimmed pretty much to one location, and the boat's course is adjusted to accommodate the change in wind direction.

In light air, station the crew a little forward of their normal position on boats with a flat run aft, as this too can help reduce wettcd surface. Shifting the weight this way lifts the wide transom out of the water, and submerges part of the narrower bow of the boat. It also helps create weather helm and, if there is a "bobble," increases the drive of the boat through the waves.

Another technique that can help drive a boat into a slop when there's no wind to speak of is to keep the crew low in the boat. This seems to reduce rolling and the boat goes faster.

CURRENT

Current, and how it affects the course of a sailboat, is often misunderstood. If three or four pieces of wood are drifting along in a current, they are essentially motionless with respect to one another. Now imagine these hunks of wood spread out in a long line parallel to the direction of the current. You could sail your boat in and out among the drifting wood much like skiing a slalom course.

If the wind were dead abeam, a boat sailing upcurrent would take no longer to complete the course than a boat sailing downcurrent. In other words, the existence of current has no real bearing on how fast a boat moves *through* the water.

One popular misconception is that current exerts more force on a deep-keeled boat than it does on a shallow draft boat. Actually, a piece of wood would stay right alongside a large cruising boat drifting along on a windless day, even if the current were running at 5 knots. The stick of wood and the cruising boat are both motionless in a moving mass of water.

Another common belief is that current on the windward side of a close-hauled boat pushes it to leeward, or current on the leeward side pushes a boat to windward through the water. This too is a lot of foolishness. The only effect current has on a boat is in relation to the way the boat moves over the ground. Nevertheless, it is mandatory for every sailor to know the direction and speed of the current, and there are numerous ways of doing this. Tide tables often are used, though in certain areas they are notoriously inaccurate. They can be as much as an hour off the actual time the tide turns, so never become overly dependent on them. A strong westerly wind (a wind blowing from the west) can delay and reduce a westerly current (one that flows from the east to the west).

The most common way to check the current is to look at it flowing by a stationary object such as a buoy. As mentioned before, the buoy will appear to be moving through the water leaving a wake; the direction of the wake will be, obviously, downcurrent. Also, watch bubbles or bits of wood or paper drift past the buoy.

If you're very familiar with a certain buoy shape, you can tell the current direction by the way it's leaning. In my experience, however, some buoys lean upcurrent and some downcurrent depending on the nature of their underwater shape and ground tackle. You must know the idiosyncrasies of the particular buoy before using its attitude to determine current direction. In a strong current, however, all buoys will lean downcurrent.

A quick look at anchored boats can also help. However, a powerboat with its high superstructure and shallow draft will usually be affected more by wind than current, so try to use an anchored deep-keeled sailboat as a guide to current direction.

During a race, constantly check the current using both of the previous methods where possible, and also use ranges. By watching land behind a buoy, you can determine whether you are holding your own against a current. Line the buoy up with an object ashore such as a tree or a house. This is called a range. If the object ashore appears to be moving slowly to the left of the buoy, you are being set to starboard, and vice versa.

Your heading may have to be well upcurrent, if the breeze is light and the current is strong, to stay on the range you've made for your boat. Ranging is used mostly on the reaching or running leg of a course. When there is no land behind the buoy to use for a range, take a compass bearing on the buoy and keep it constant. This is the same idea as a collision course. If the bearing doesn't change, you will collide, or in this case, reach the buoy by having sailed the shortest possible distance. If there is no land and you don't have a compass, look back at the buoy you came from, then look forward to the next one and judge whether you're still on a straight line between them. If not, adjust your course accordingly.

The depth of water has a great deal to do with the speed of the current. There's an old saying: "Still water runs deep." Not so with currents. Still water really runs shallow. The swiftest current is found where water is the deepest. The one exception to this is where water depth is only slightly shallower than surrounding deep water. Here, water will speed up to cross the shallow spot rather than find its way around it. If you look at the water depths on a chart, you can determine where to sail to get into faster current or where to sail to avoid it, depending on your own course relative to it.

Look at waves a few hundred yards offshore or where you know the water begins to get deeper. If they are shorter in length and choppier than waves farther inshore, the current is running against the wind. Since you know wind direction, you easily can determine the current direction.

Whether you want to stay in the chop depends on whether the current will be with you or against you and whether you are beating or running. On a beat, this chop may slow the boat enough so that the advantages of such a favorable current are actually offset.

Though current has no effect on how a boat moves through the water in relation to another boat, it has a large effect on how the boat moves over the bottom. This causes confusion among some sailors about what "lee-bow" current does to a boat. Many feel that if they can point high enough to get the current on the leeward side of their bow, they will get a boost to windward with the current. Figure 8-1 shows why it appears that way. Boats A and B are even at the start. Boat A sails normally while Boat B pinches. Thus at positions A1 and B1 without current, Boat A is ahead of B, but B has squeezed out to windward a bit. Now inject current into this picture. Boat A is dead into it and ends up in position A2. Boat B has the current on her lee bow and ends up in position B2—the same amount behind and to windward of her first position as she would have been were there no current at all. If you draw in apparent wind vectors, you'll find that the current affects the apparent wind the same for each boat. Actually, the current is creating a new direction and velocity of true wind for all boats sailing in the same current, and it's the individual boat's course and speed that is creating its own particular apparent wind. Therefore, Figure 8-1 isn't perfectly accurate as it shows only one wind direction with or without current, but the effect is the same. About the only advantage Boat B has over

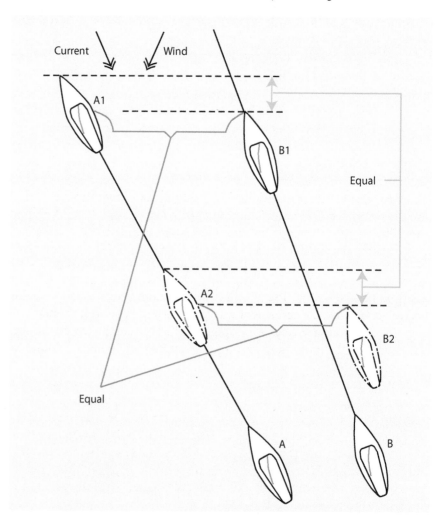

Figure 8-1. Pinching to *lee bow,* the current doesn't give you any advantage over pinching when there is no current.

Boat A is if B, by pinching, has been able to fetch a mark, whereas A has had to make two tacks. In light air this can be very time-consuming.

If the wind is very light and you have a strong contrary current, be well aware that you may be sailing backward. At night it is particularly hard to know that this is happening, but when you've made the correct diagnosis, it's extremely rewarding (in relation to other boats) to anchor. (Yes, anchor, even in a race!) Many times we've anchored and found ourselves moving "up" past the running lights of other competitors who have failed to anchor. The current is setting them backward in relation to us, and their reaction is that we have a little more wind than they. A range of a buoy against the land, two lights ashore, or a compass bearing to a known landmark will help tip you off that you're losing ground against the current. Of course, we now have GPS to tell us the effect of the current.

When it becomes necessary to anchor during daylight hours in a small-boat race, slip the anchor over the side as surreptitiously as possible, preferably to leeward. If your competitors don't see you do it, you may gain quite a margin on them by the time they figure it out and sort out their anchor line. When anchored, lend all credence possible to the fact that you are still sailing the boat as fast as you can make it go. Crew may be to leeward sitting on the anchor line as it leads over the side from the cockpit. The main and jib are being tended properly and the skipper steering with the appearance of utmost concentration.

The time to get the anchor up is before the line tends aft. When there's enough wind to sail forward and get slack in the anchor line, make the decision whether it's a temporary puff or a lasting breeze. If the latter, get the anchor up in a hurry. In doing so you'll be giving the boat a little boost forward, and there's nothing illegal about that. You just don't want to wait so long that the boat is past the anchor and by raising the anchor you will slow the boat up.

The late Peter Barrett was a brilliant sailor and one of the best talents our country has ever had. He told a story of two guys, let's call them Bob and Joe, who lived on a river several miles up current north of a bridge. They bet each other who could sail down to the bridge in the fastest time on Saturday. The current was five knots in a southerly direction. Bob knew that a light five-knot north wind was predicted Saturday morning and decided to sail in the morning. Joe hoped for a much stronger wind in the afternoon, so he waited. The wind pooped out completely at noon, but Joe had to go, because the agreement was for Saturday. Who won the bet?

Joe did. Bob's five-knot wind was cancelled out completely by the five-knot speed of the boat downcurrent. The apparent wind on his boat was zero, so the sails didn't help. But for Joe, the five-knot current created a five-knot apparent wind dead ahead, so he merrily tacked back and forth down-current, sailed faster than the current, and easily beat Bob's time.

I had a real-time example of the same unusual process in England for the Admiral's Cup during Cowes Week on a 48' sloop named *Carina* in 1971. Before the start of one of the races, there was no wind and a strong current setting the fleet across the starting line prematurely. The owner asked me how to play the start. Since the rules stated you have to cut your engine five minutes before the start, I suggested we power upcurrent to a position we thought would be five minutes of drifting to the starting line and cut the engine. We did, but found ourselves drifting stern first to the line. We saw one boat turned properly with its bow heading downcurrent. The speed of the current created wind in their sails, so they moved out on the fleet.

Our exasperated skipper asked for suggestions to turn our bow downcurrent. I grabbed the anchor from belowdecks, and we dropped it over the stern so it just touched bottom. The drag caused the boat to rotate so the stern was upcurrent. We then hoisted the anchor back on board, trimmed our sails, and were the second boat out of the pack. We earned a second place in the sailing race.

SAFETY

Be very aware of areas of possible weakness on a large sailboat. Avoid walking to leeward of the mainsail boom, particularly in the vicinity of the gooseneck. And be careful not to step in the bight of a snatchblock, so that, if the shackle holding the block gives way, the block becomes the rock of a slingshot. I was sailing on an 82' maxi yacht practicing in about 20 knots of wind for the Sydney–Hobart Race in Sydney Harbor. We set a spinnaker and it was not filling, so, as tactician, I suggested to the owner to head up a few degrees to fill the spinnaker. He did and it filled with a bang. A crew member amidships was standing in the coil of the lazy guy and the wire guy parted. He was pulled up around the headstay, some 40 feet away, and then overboard. We were all aghast, but we tossed the life-saving equipment over the side. Luckily, a photo boat reached the crew member and grabbed him by the hair as he was going down. He had compound fractures of his legs and many other injuries. The lesson learned is be careful where you step, replace running rigging before it gets tired, and practice crew overboard procedures, so reactions are automatic no matter how stressful the situation is.

We sailed our own boat *Sleuth*, a 54' sloop, in the infamous 1979 Fastnet Race where 19 sailors died. At the height of the storm I estimated 25-foot waves and 85-knot winds. All the crew were wearing harnesses, at that time a newly invented safety product consisting of a belt with shoulder straps and a tether line with a snapshackle to snap on to a solid fixture or onto jack lines (safety lines running from the bow to the stern that you can snap on once and cover the whole distance). If a wave washes you overboard, you will still be attached. Under the conditions, with waves washing into our cockpit, I added a rule: if a crew member was going below, they had to do it while attached and then ask a crew member on deck to unsnap his/her tether. Conversely, when coming up on deck, he/she had to pass his/her tether up to someone on deck to snap on. A few years later I read accounts of a real buster on the Sydney–Hobart Race, where a crew member unsnapped his harness to go below, was washed over the side by a wave, and lost.

Some accidents occur when a bow crew tries to snap the tack corner of the spinnaker free for a takedown. Released from the strain, the spinnaker pole snaps backward and woe be the head that is in the way. I once saw a crew member's head right next to the pole as he reached to pop the spinnaker tack off. I yelled "duck" and thank god he had fast reactions. The pole grazed his head.

TEST QUESTIONS

1. What is the most important factor in steering that makes one helmsman better than another?
2. Where should crew weight be in drifting conditions?
3. Does current run faster in deeper or shallower water?
4. How can you judge what effect the current is having on your boat?
5. What is "lee-bow" current?

Chapter 9

Safety and Emergencies

OBSERVING WEAKNESSES

Safety is both the prevention of emergencies and the preparation for them, when and if they occur. It may take years of experience, but some people are able to develop a sixth sense of when something is not quite right. For instance, I went for a one-hour sail to check out some new jibs for my 54' ocean racer *Sleuth*. It was my first sail in six months, and I noticed that someone had shackled on one of the mainsheet blocks a quarter turn from lining up properly with the sheet pull. If it had been blowing harder and we had trimmed the sheet in tightly, we would have twisted, weakened, and possibly broken the bale on which the block was attached. We immediately corrected it, and not five minutes later I noticed someone had used a bolt with a nonlocking nut on our starboard running backstay. If the nut came off and the bolt popped out, we could have lost the mast. These seem like small things to notice and an untrained eye would miss them completely, but they were important. Knowing what the end result might be if they had not been corrected comes from long experience and training.

In fact, some sailors never seem to be able to develop this sixth sense, although much of it is no mystery. You've seen something break before and you look out for it. A few years ago I advised an Olympic contender that he'd better change his spinnaker halyard shackle before competing in the final races. Sure enough, it broke the next day in a practice race. I just happened to know it was a weak design.

I could give you hundreds of examples, but I doubt that would help the reader because each boat and event is a little different. Suffice it to say many emergencies can be avoided by being observant. Here are some of the things to look for:

1. Corrosion or hairline splits in shroud swage fittings that attach to the turnbuckles.
2. A broken strand on a shroud or stay.
3. Evidence of chafe on rope halyards, burrs on wire halyards.
4. Excessive water in the bilge, corrosion around through-hull fittings.
5. A captive pin halyard shackle that needs spreading to keep the pin from flopping around. (You should need to squeeze the sides of the shackle to insert the pin.)
6. Lack of seizing wire on anchor shackles.

7. Sharp untaped cotter pins that can rip sails.
8. Sharp edges on the boom that can also rip sails.
9. Loose or funny-feeling steering.
10. Loose shackle pins on important items like hiking straps. If they let go, you can end up overboard.
11. No cotter pins in shroud turnbuckles (often forgotten by the person tuning the rig, with possible loss of the mast resulting).
12. Note loss of cotter pins from any clevis pins you see.
13. Signs of weakness in the area of the main boom gooseneck. This is an area of tremendous strain and can be dangerous if the boom breaks free.
14. Ensure that the covers for any "watertight" compartments are securely fastened in case the cockpit fills with water.
15. Any loose deck blocks, travelers, or winches indicate that the nuts on some of the through-bolts have backed off. Any undue strain on the block might cause it to pop off the deck.
16. A bad lead on an anchor line or mooring line may cause chafe and the loss of your boat hours after you've left it for the night.
17. Broken stitching in a batten pocket. Small tears in a sail.

Most of the above are found on small boats. With cruising boats there are myriad other things that can go wrong because a larger boat brings far greater strains, engine and electrical problems, and dinghy and propeller tangling problems, among others.

The old adage "an ounce of prevention is worth a pound of cure" is especially apropos on a boat. So before you go out, try to spot the various potential sources of eventual emergencies and correct them.

HANDLING EMERGENCIES

Let's imagine that you have not noticed the signs of trouble before going out sailing for the day. Certain emergencies occur. How do you handle them?

Shrouds

The first situation occurs because you didn't notice the cracks in the swaged fitting on your starboard upper shroud. It breaks when you are on a starboard tack, and the mast bends perilously to leeward. Immediately spin the boat into the wind, dumping air out of the mainsail and jib and flipping over to the port tack. This puts the pressure on the unbroken port shrouds and saves the mast. If you can't go on port tack for some reason such as proximity to shore, shoot into the wind, get your sails down, and anchor. If a wire shroud breaks and the break is near the turnbuckle and you have some U-bolts aboard, you can make another eye and reattach the turnbuckle, assuming it's a small sailboat. Or you can take both ends of the spinnaker halyard out to the edge of the deck and fasten it securely. If it's a double-ended halyard and one end is still attached to the mast, stretch can cause poor support, so attach both ends to the deck edge. If possible, shinny up the mast and pull the halyard out to the spreader tip with a looped line so the spreader can help support the mast as it does with the upper shroud.

Backstay

Occasionally the backstay breaks on a sailboat. If it happens when running downwind, the mast could fall forward over the bow because of the pull of the spinnaker and the mainsail. The first thing to do if the backstay breaks is to throw off the spinnaker sheet and round up into the wind immediately. Get the spinnaker down and luff the mainsail and jib immediately. This takes the pressure off the sails, and wind resistance pushes the mast and rigging toward the stern of the boat. Then trim in the mainsail tight. The leech of the mainsail on a small boat will almost have the same holding power as the backstay. Note the number of parts on the mainsheet and the strength with which you haul it in. Make sure the traveler is centered in the middle of the boat for maximum mast support. In moderate winds you can sail on most points of sail with the main trimmed in as if close-hauled. In heavier winds the main can be reefed down quite far and still give some support and allow you to sail to a destination. However, the support will only be to the point where the head of the sail is on the mast. To support the upper part of the mast, secure the spinnaker halyard aft at the stern (on boats where the spinnaker halyard runs to the top of the mast).

Another option in heavy winds is to douse the mainsail and run the main halyard either to the end of the boom or to the stem. By attaching the main halyard to the end of the boom, cleating the other end, and trimming the mainsheet tightly, we get excellent mast support. Attach the halyard to a boom bale, not the outhaul, because the latter can break. On larger sailboats with a main halyard winch, shackle the halyard right to the stern of the boat (or to an extra line if the halyard isn't long enough), and tension it tightly by use of the winch.

Headstay

Usually when a headstay breaks, the crew has a little time before the mast falls backward because the jib luff will support it for awhile. The proper maneuver is to head downwind and ease the mainsail immediately. The force of the wind in the mainsail will push the mast forward and keep it standing. It's also fairly easy to find another unused halyard (either spinnaker or spare jib halyard on many boats) to attach to the bow for temporary support. When you get into the harbor, lower the mainsail first and then take care of the jib.

Spreaders

Sometimes the windward spreader breaks. The same procedures apply as when a shroud breaks. Tack or jibe immediately to put the strain on the good spreader on the other side of the mast. If you can sail on that tack back to the harbor, you don't have to worry about repairing the spreader.

More often, though, you have to make repairs in order to be able to sail on the initial tack with the broken spreader. Search around the boat for a piece of wood or tubing with which to splint the spreader. On small boats, remember there's a tiller extension, oar, or other things that might be used. If you're desperate, even the tiller could be used. Then steer with the sails and a pair of pliers or Vise-Grips attached to the rudderhead. The key to survival in any situation is to be as inventive as possible.

Rudder

In the case of a lost rudder, there is no way to replace it. On a larger boat there are usually tools available to attach a floorboard to one end of the spinnaker pole and the other end to the transom, thereby creating a sweep oar for steering, but even this is not as effective as steering the boat with the sails alone. Just trim and cleat the jib. Then play the mainsail, easing it to head off and trimming it to head up. Put crew weight to windward to head off, to leeward to head up. To tack, free the jib and trim the main. Then, when head to wind, back the jib to make sure the bow gets completely across the eye of the wind. Jibing can only be done in light winds: ease the mainsail out completely and back the jib to windward to force the bow down to a run. Then get all the crew weight way out over the windward side to increase lee helm. The main should swing over to the other jibe, but don't trim it in after it does because the boat will round up and could go into a broach.

Sinking

Sinking is not a common emergency, thank God, but it can happen that the boat fills up with water to the extent that sinking is a possibility. If a small boat broaches on a spinnaker run and a crew releases the spinnaker guy, the spinnaker may lay the boat over flat and it's likely the cockpit will fill with water. With the forward and aft hatches closed, there should be no problem. Get the spinnaker down and luff the sails so the boat straightens up. Then bail like crazy with buckets. I like to have at least one bucket on any boat I sail. A cruising boat should have many. Pumps do a good job, but they are unreliable as debris can clog the intake. Moreover, only one crew member can usually pump whereas many can bail with buckets.

While sailing with the boat full of water, head for shallow water so the boat will be easily recoverable if it sinks. Under no circumstances should you make any violent alteration of course. I once saw a boat that was full of water sailing on a reach toward the shore. The helmsman decided to round up into the wind and stop the boat in order to bail more efficiently. The boat turned, but the water in the boat kept on going in the original direction of travel. The weight and force of the water rolled the boat flat over. It filled the rest of the way and sank.

In such conditions the crew should already have life vests on. When it's obvious that there's nothing that can be done to avoid sinking, try to tie a fender or some floating item to a long line such as a spinnaker sheet to mark the location of the boat for salvage later. You'd be surprised how much time you actually have. Air is usually trapped under the deck, and the last throes are really quite slow as the bow or stem finally disappears beneath the waves. Make sure that the crew is well clear of the boat and in no way entangled in the various lines as she sinks.

Many daysailers have forward and aft compartments. As long as they are tight, the boat will float. However, a collision with another boat can result in a hole in one of the compartments. I saw such a collision puncture the aft compartment on a racing boat. On one tack the hole was submerged; on the other it was out of the water. The obvious procedure is to stay on the tack that keeps the hole out of the water until temporary repairs can be made. This particular crew didn't do that. Then one of the crew members opened up the aft compartment hatch to see if he could plug the hole from the inside. The effort was well-intentioned, but misguided. Water poured into the cockpit from the compartment, and the crew barely got the hatch refastened. If the cockpit had also fIlled with water, the boat couldn't have remained afloat.

There are a few things that can be done about a hole under the waterline in a boat. First stuff clothes or blankets in the hole. Next cover it from the outside with plastic and then cover the plastic with a blanket or sails fixed in place with lines that go right under the boat and tie to either side. (This is called a collision mat.) I have never had to resort to this, and I hope I never will. The water pressure is said to hold the collision mat in place, but I'll believe it's a practical solution when I've had to try it. Nevertheless, it doesn't hurt to have some kind of solution in mind for emergencies that have never happened to you.

SQUALLS

Squalls are small, local, often unforecast storms. They often form on hot summer days as a result of nearby land heating up. This causes the air to rise and large cumulus clouds to form. These thunderheads are often anvil shaped and quite dark down low. There may be almost no wind as a squall approaches, and suddenly you're met by a strong blast coming out of it. Then, as it passes, the wind will shift—often as much as 180°.

Other types of squalls are associated with frontal passages and can be fairly accurately forecast. If the weather forecast has predicted a front to pass, you may expect some prefrontal squalls in the neighborhood.

Judging Intensity

The problem for sailors is to determine beforehand just how intense the squall will be. Quite often the experience you have had from past squalls in a given location will suggest what to expect for future ones. For instance, when a nasty-looking squall hit us once or twice a winter in the Bahamas, it was as bad as it looked: blowing 60 with a driving rain. In the Virgin Islands, a squall that looked exactly the same as it approached rarely had over 35-knot winds. The result is that I view a squall with a great deal more caution in the Bahamas than in the Virgins. Yet nothing is absolute and many squalls have the potential of great damage. Near Captiva Island, Florida, a squall's intensity can be deceiving. We were hit by one squall a few winters ago that developed into a twister five miles after it passed us, knocking over house trailers on nearby Pine Island.

It's best to treat any approaching squall with respect. Look for signs that might measure its force and don't be fooled too much by darkness. On a bright sunny day a low bank of clouds in the distance casts a shadow underneath that looks very ominous. Yet when the bank arrives, there's nothing there except a solid blanket of low-lying clouds instead of the sun you had previously. Had you shortened sail because of it, you'd have felt very foolish. Without any vertical development of the clouds, there's not apt to be much increase in wind velocity.

The squalls I get concerned about are those that stand out as very dark on an already overcast day, which means the cloud layer is very thick right down close to the water surface. Often there's a pink tinge underneath that I can't account for, but when you see the pink tinge—watch out! It's apt to be a dilly. Obvious white caps in the distance also warn you of a high-intensity squall. If you're lucky enough to have other boats between you and the squall, watch how the winds affect them. If you see them knocked flat by the squall, quickly shorten or douse sail yourself. If they just disappear into the darkness of the squall without appearing to be affected by it, don't be lulled into believing the squall has no power. After the boats disappear from your sight, it's possible they might be hit by a blast. However, if there's no strong wind visible on initial entry into the squall, there's not apt to be much wind farther into it.

Preparation

In small keelboats without foam flotation, the proper way to prepare for a squall is to first make sure that the flotation compartments are fastened securely closed. All crew should put on life vests, then get the anchor out and coil the line properly so it can run freely.

It is important that you set up the anchor line so that it runs out from the bow. To do so, take the bitter end of the line and run it through the bow eye and aft to the mast. Wrap the line twice around the mast and tie a bowline. Now overhaul the line through the bow eye and coil it neatly in the cockpit. Do this before the squall hits, because getting up on the foredeck in the middle of the squall could be very dangerous. If you slipped overboard, there's no way the crew could come back to pick you up if the squall was an extremely violent one. Anchoring from the cockpit in the middle of a squall, without leading the line to the bow, will cause great complications. The boat will be broadside to the seas, which will put a great strain on the anchor, the line, and the point of attachment to the boat. Something will have to give. If it holds for a while, the waves will smash against the side of the boat and fill up the cockpit.

If you are certain you can sail back into the harbor before the squall hits, that's the best solution to the squall management problem. Don't attempt it if you are not certain. Nothing's worse than being hit by the squall in an area of restricted mobility surrounded by shoals. It's far better to get away from shallow water, even if it means heading away from the harbor, if you can't get safely inside before it hits.

Dousing Sails

The first sail to lower is the largest one. On most small boats it's the mainsail. When the first blast hits, the mainsail will lay you over (if it hasn't been doused) and easing the mainsheet doesn't help much. The boom hits the water because of the heeling of the boat and pushes it in just when you want to ease it more. With the mainsail unable to be eased, the heeling increases and eventually the boat will swamp—the cockpit will fill with water.

So get the mainsail down. Assign emergency positions so each person knows his or her specific task: releasing the mainsheet, boom vang, and cunningham, or unhooking the halyard while holding the boom up to free the leech. Remember that all tasks are much more difficult to perform when it's very windy, so allow a little extra time. Be sure to take the halyard off the mainsail so it can't accidentally fly out like a spinnaker attached only by the head and foot. Then flake the mainsail on the boom as neatly as possible, wrap the head around all the flakes once or twice, and tie the whole sail snugly with the mainsheet.

With only the jib up in heavy winds, you will be able to sail as high as a beam reach, but it is doubtful that you will be able to make any headway to windward. The stronger the wind becomes, the more you will have to run before it. If running before it at high speed is not getting you anywhere advantageous, you will probably want to reduce speed by dousing the jib and running "under bare poles." If your boat does not have jib roller furling, lower the jib and keep both jib sheets tight as the sail comes down so the clew is centered right in front of the mast and the foot is stretched taut. Reach forward and tuck the body of the sail under the foot to avoid having much of the sail go over the side. If possible try to wrap the spinnaker pole foreguy or the ends of the jib sheets around the sail to furl it. Don't go up on the foredeck. Stay in the cockpit, and if you can't get the jib neatly rolled up and secured, don't worry about it. As long as the foot is tight and the sail is well lowered, you won't have too much trouble.

If you're still traveling too fast on a larger boat or if you're in water too deep to anchor, consider dragging a warp or sea anchor off the stern. A warp is just a towline without the tow. Resistance can be added to it by attaching sail bags or a bucket or by just adding more line, thus making it longer.

Anchoring

All this is fine where there's plenty of sea room, but in the presence of land or shoals, movement over the bottom must be reduced or stopped. This is where our anchoring preparations come in. Double-check that the anchor lines won't wrap around anything such as someone's leg as it runs out. With a good head of speed, round up into the wind and lower the anchor over the side. Since you have overhauled the line aft of the bow eye, you can wrap it around the jib sheet winch and pay it out. This should be done relatively smartly. Using the jib winch allows you to increase the scope more slowly after the anchor has a good bite. It avoids the possibility of breaking the line, which could happen if you tossed all the line overboard and waited for the anchor to bite and the boat to reach the end of the line with one gigantic jerk. Remember there are presumably heavy seas running and the boat could be surging down one of these seas when the end of the line was reached. Moreover, paying the line out under control keeps the bow headed into the seas, thereby offering less resistance to the waves. And lastly, the chance of someone or something getting caught in the line zinging out is diminished.

Both now, and particularly when underway, keep the boat as dry as possible. Water in the boat makes the boat sluggish to handle and lowers the freeboard. Waves are able to come over the side more easily the lower she gets, and soon you won't be able to keep up with the waves.

Heaving-to

Heaving-to is a handy thing to know about and practice, whether you want to stop sailing for a while and relax for lunch or some other activity, or if you're caught in a violent storm. Back the jib to the windward side and cleat it. Since the mainsail will be forcing the boat forward and up into the wind and the jib will be forcing the boat backward and the bow down away from the wind, an equilibrium can be maintained. The tiller or wheel can be tied or locked in the position that best augments the equilibrium—usually to leeward. The boat will move very slowly through the water making quite a bit of leeway depending on the wind strength.

The easiest way is to start on port tack close-hauled and to tack without releasing the jib sheet. Now you have backed the jib and are on starboard tack with right-of-way over any other port tack boat that may approach while you are relaxing or having lunch. Next ease the mainsail until your speed dies and steer toward the backed jib by tying the tiller or locking the wheel to leeward with the mainsail luffing.

A friend of mine has sailed thousands of miles with just his wife on a keel-centerboard cruising boat. When a storm hits, he reefs the main, heaves-to, and raises the centerboard. The boat makes such rapid leeway that it leaves a flat "wake" to windward that seems to level oncoming breaking waves. He and his wife then go below and play cards for a day or two until the storm passes, enjoying relative comfort without being tossed around by the seas.

GROUNDINGS

Sooner or later anyone who sails will go aground. Though often embarrassing, generally it's not dangerous unless it's the windward side of a reef. More often the bottom is sand or mud in a bay or sound, and you've hit because you were sailing too close to shore in order to get out of the current, a sand bar shifted from its position on the chart, or you weren't following your course on the chart closely enough. With a centerboard boat it's easy. Once you bump, raise the centerboard and head for deeper water.

A boat with a keel is a bit more difficult. The most important reaction when you first hit is to heel the boat immediately. Trim in the sails flat and get all your crew weight to leeward. More acrobatic crew members can walk out on the boom, as it's eased out over the water, leaning against the windward side of the mainsail. Others can hang on the leeward shrouds. Try to sway the boat by leaning in and then way out. By getting the boat to roll, the swing to leeward will be greater than by weight alone.

If this doesn't work use the spinnaker pole to push off. This method is good if the bottom is hard, but with a muddy bottom, the pole just sinks into the mud. Plus it fouls up the jaws and springs in the pole with dried mud, rendering them useless for their designed purpose at a later time.

Another answer is to bite the bullet and get wet. Say your boat draws 4'6". If you're hard aground, the water is only about three feet deep. Get over the side and start shoving. Rotate the boat by pushing the bow from one side while someone else pushes the stern. For better purchase, take the anchor over the side and carry it out the full length of the anchor rode into deeper water. Even when the water gets deeper than your height, you can move the anchor out away from the boat. Rest the anchor on the bottom and with the line vertical, lift and swim. Wear a life vest to increase your buoyancy and for safety. Be careful if there is a strong current that can carry you away from the boat. If the anchor isn't very heavy (and it's much lighter underwater), you should be able to move it. Back on the boat, wrap the anchor line around a jib sheet winch and crank. You can achieve tremendous pulling power in this manner and may very well pull the boat off. This is called "kedging off."

Obviously another method is to accept some friendly assistance from a powerboat. I would suggest that you determine beforehand if there will be a charge and, if so, how much it will be. Some "helpful" people try to charge for their services afterward. Use your own line rather than accepting one from the powerboat. I understand that, under Admiralty Law, salvage can be more readily claimed and hold up in court if you accept a tow line from the towboat rather than tossing yours.

When a couple of powerboats are helping, it's sometimes practical to have one pull on a halyard to heel the boat over farther while the other pulls on the hull. Do NOT do this on a boat with an unsupported mast. We have lost two masts because well-meaning rescuers pulled on the main halyard (after the mainsail was doused) on our Soling sailboats. The Soling mast is completely unsupported above the upper shrouds except for the backstay. Any side pull on the main halyard will break the upper part off. Also some masts on smaller boats, regardless of how strongly supported by stays, can't take the unusual force and direction of a powerboat pulling it over. Use this method only on a cruising boat.

DISTRESS SIGNALS

Most of us are aware of the normal distress signals such as the "SOS" signal ("Save Our Ship"): •••---••• in Morse Code. There are many other official distress signals listed in the International Rules of the Road:

- A gun or other explosive signal fired at intervals of about a minute.
- A continuous sounding with any fog-signalling apparatus.
- Rockets or shells, throwing red stars, fired one at a time at short intervals.
- A signal sent by radio-telephone consisting of the spoken word "MAYDAY." This comes from the French "m'aider" meaning "help me." "MAYDAY" is only used when you are in grave and immediate lethal danger to person or property. If not in distress, use the "urgent" signal "PAN" repeated three times. Don't forget to radio your position.
- The International Code Signal of distress indicated by flying the flags "N" over "C."
- A signal consisting of a square flag having above or below it a ball or anything resembling a ball.
- Flames on the vessel (as from a burning tar barrel, oil barrel, etc.).

Figure 9-1. Official distress signals as listed in the International Rules of the Road.

- A rocket parachute flare or a hand flare showing a red light.
- A smoke signal giving off orange-colored smoke.
- Slowly and repeatedly raising and lowering arms outstretched each side.
- The radio telegraph alarm signal. Signals transmitted by emergency position-indicating radio beacon (commonly known as EPIRB).

I used to believe that an upside-down ensign or flag was a signal of distress but it's not on the official list.

COLLISIONS

If you have taken a boating or sailing course, you have learned the basic right-of-way rules. Let's briefly review them.

After many years of substantial differences, the Inland and International Rules of the Road are now, for all intents and purposes, identical. We have three possibilities: sail versus sail, sail versus power, and power versus power.

When you are sailing and meet another sailboat you are either: 1) on opposite tacks, 2) on the same tack, or 3) overtaking or being overtaken. On opposite tacks, the starboard tack boat has right-of-way. On the same tack, the leeward boat has right-of-way. In an overtaking situation, the overtaking boat must avoid hitting the overtaken boat.

When you are sailing and meet a boat under power, you have right-of-way in almost all cases. The few exceptions are when the motorboat is anchored or not under command, is fishing, is being overtaken by the sailboat, or when the motorboat is a large vessel, such as a ship or tug and barge, restricted in her ability to maneuver.

When you are under power and meet another powerboat, the one in the other's "danger zone" has right of way. The danger zone is the area from dead ahead to two points (22.5°) abaft the starboard beam. In simpler terms, when there is any risk of collision, the boat approaching from the right has right of way. Remember a sailboat under power, even if the sails are up, is a motorboat, according to the Rules of the Road. Any sailing vessel has to stay out of the way of a commercial vessel in a narrow channel when the latter can safely maneuver only in that channel.

In all the above cases, the boat with the right of way is the "stand-on" vessel. The boat that has to avoid the collision is the "give-way" vessel. The stand-on vessel must maintain her course and speed to avoid misleading the vessel giving way, but must, nevertheless, avoid a collision when it appears the give-way vessel is unable to fulfill her obligations to keep clear.

The important part, no matter which boat you are, is to determine very early if the chance of a collision exists. A collision will occur if the bearing between the two boats doesn't change. If we maintain a steady, constant course and line up something such as a shroud with the converging boat and the shroud continues to line up with the other boat minutes later, a collision can result. Or if we take a compass bearing, a more accurate method, and the bearing doesn't change as the boats get closer together, watch out for a potential collision. But let me recommend a very practical and simple method to achieve the same thing. The only requirement to use this system is that there be land a mile or so behind the other boat. As you converge with the other boat, watch the relationship between the other boat and the land. If the other boat appears to be moving forward past the land, she will cross you. If the other boat appears to be losing ground on the land, you will cross her. But if she remains stationary against the land, you are on a collision course. The crew will generally watch the other boat and tell the skipper that he or she is gaining ("making land") or losing.

The biggest cause of collisions and near misses is inattentiveness. Sailors get notoriously lulled into a sense of solitude. Even in fairly crowded waters the sea gives a feeling of spaciousness. Sailboats travel very slowly compared to the high speed we're used to on the highways, so we don't have the same feeling of a need for alertness. Yet two boats a mile apart each sailing at six knots can hit each other in five minutes. An all too common comment after a near miss is, "Where the devil did he come from?" The boat was always there, but unnoticed. This is a very good reson why drinking and sailing don't mix. Save the drinking for after you're anchored and not expecting to go sailing again that day.

Night Collisions

It's not unusual for the breeze to die around dusk, and sailors who have ventured too far away from home may find themselves caught out after sundown. Make sure, therefore, that your boat has all the necessary lights and emergency flares for night sailing. A small sailboat under 20 meters (roughly 65') must have red and green sidelights, but they may be combined on the centerline. There are a number of flashlight battery types on the market for small sailboats. A stern light is also required, and it's a good idea to have a fairly strong battery-powered spotlight aboard.

Probably the largest concern after dark is being run down by a commercial vessel such as a tugboat with a tow. A few years ago, in Long Island Sound, a motoryacht was struck by a barge being towed by a tug, and five lives were lost. It behooves you to understand the lights on tugs because the tows are often far behind the tugboat, and weakly lit. If you mistakenly sail in front of the tow at night you're out of luck. The tow can't swerve to avoid you, nor can it stop on its own. It's even unlikely that there is anyone riding on the towed barge, so there's no one to see the accident and call for help. Plus the tug's crew, sometimes 300 yards (three football field lengths) ahead, is not apt to see or hear anything at night. It's crucial, therefore, to correctly establish whether there is a barge. The rule is simple. If the tow is more than 200 meters behind, the tug carries three 225° masthead white lights arranged vertically on a staff and a yellow towing light above the stern light. If the tow is less than 200 meters back, you will see two vertical lights and a yellow towing light. If the tow is alongside the tug, two vertical white lights are shown, but no yellow towing light. These are in addition to the normal side lights, and stern light. Where there are no white lights arranged vertically, there is no tow and you can safely pass astern of the tug. There will be a masthead light forward and a higher one aft of it as in most other powerboats.

Let's say you see a boat on a collision course with the normal lights plus a green light over a white light vertically. This is a trawler dragging nets and has right of way over you. There are a number of other types of vessels with unusual lights you may encounter out at night. If you can't identify them, the safest procedure is to take compass bearings to determine if you're on a collision course. If you are, make a large alteration of course to stay away from them. There's a saying, "He was right, dead right, as he sailed along, and now he's as dead as if he'd been wrong." Don't push your right-of-way, especially at night.

When it appears that there may be a close call developing, and the other vessel may not be aware of your existence, the spotlight mentioned previously can come in handy. The traditional method to display your presence has been to flash the light up on your sails to illuminate them for the vessel's skipper to see. I've found this works well on nights with a good visibility but is next to useless in bad conditions (when you most need to be seen). Shine the spotlight right at the wheelhouse of the vessel. From this vantage the battery-operated spotlight will look like a pinprick of light, if they see it at all. It certainly won't blind the helmsman, which you obviously want to avoid, but will enable them to see that there's a boat out there they may not have been aware of.

Many people use binoculars during the day and tend to forget that a good set of binoculars can save a great deal of inner stress at dusk or at night. I was in a situation one time where we were converging with a number of commercial boats and it was hard to know exactly what they were doing. The lights seemed confusing. By checking with binoculars we found we could cross one tug towing a barge and sail between it and another tug towing a barge to windward of the first tug and tow. Until we used binoculars, we couldn't tell who was towing what. In another situation we were converging at dusk with a ship that was all lit up like a Christmas tree. We couldn't pick out the side lights and had no idea which way it was going, A check with binoculars showed it to be a large sailing schooner with a generator that accounted for all the lights, and we easily set a course to avoid her. You can also use the VHF radio to contact the other vessel on Channel 16 or 13. Commercial operators will welcome the chance to clarify their position and intention.

TEST QUESTIONS

1. If a shroud breaks, what is the first thing to do?
2. To steer without a rudder, how do you head off?
3. What can happen if you quickly turn a boat that's full of water?
4. What indicates an intense squall?
5. What do three vertical lights on a powerboat indicate to you?
6. Which sail is doused first in a squall?
7. What is a "warp"?
8. What is "kedging"?
9. What is the Morse Code distress signal?
10. What is the origin of the word "Mayday"?

Answers to Test Questions

CHAPTER 1

1. What is the "draft" of a sail? *The maximum depth of the sail.*
2. What is a "cunningham"? *A device to pull down on the luff of a mainsail.*
3. What is "twist" in a sail? *The falling off of the leech of the sail.*
4. How can you use the mainsheet and the traveler to increase twist? *Put the traveler to windward and ease the mainsheet.*
5. What is "mast rake" versus "mast bend"? *Mast rake leans the whole mast aft. Mast bend is a bend in the middle of the mast.*
6. Is a sail with a free leech fuller or flatter than one with a tight leech? *Flatter.*
7. What controls twist in a jib? *Jib sheet.*
8. Are flat sails for speed or for power? *Speed.*
9. What are the threads called that run lengthwise in sailcloth? *Warp.*

CHAPTER 2

1. Does heeling to windward increase or decrease weather helm on a run? *Decrease.*
2. What is "roll tacking"? *Using crew weight to keep air in the sails throughout a tack.*
3. Should you tack at the crest or the trough of a wave in heavy air? *Crest.*
4. What is "wetted surface"? *The square foot area in contact with the water.*
5. What is "pumping" a sail? *Pulling in a sail quickly and repeatedly to create forward motion.*

CHAPTER 3

1. What is chord? Draft? *Chord is the distance from luff to leech. Draft is the maximum depth of a sail.*
2. What does the traveler do? *A traveler changes the angle of attack of the mainsail without changing the mainsheet tension.*
3. Does backstay tension "cock" or "free" the leech of the main? *Free.*
4. Does raking the mast effectively move the jib lead forward or aft? *Aft.*
5. What is "turning the sail inside out"? *Excessive mast bend.*
6. Should the sails be full or flat in heavy airs and large seas? *Full.*
7. What is a "balanced" rudder? *Rudder post is about a third of the way aft to offset lift.*
8. What happens to the apparent wind in a puff? *Goes aft.*
9. What happens to the apparent wind when a boat suddenly surfs? *Goes forward.*

CHAPTER 4

1. What's the last thing to do before pulling the spinnaker up? *Check the halyard is clear.*
2. Should you head up to fill the sail when you have a wrap? *No.*
3. If the spinnaker collapses with a jib set, what should you do about the jib? *Ease it and douse it if it happens again.*
4. What does easing the spinnaker halyard do? When should it be eased? *It gets the spinnaker*

Answers to Test Questions

away from the mainsail. On a medium-air reach.

5. To help avoid broaching, should crew weight be forward or aft? *Aft.*
6. If the spinnaker halyard is eased a little, will rolling be more aggravated or more controlled? *More aggravated.*
7. In light air should the spinnaker pole be lower or higher than the rest of the sail generally? *Higher.*
8. Should the foredeck crew face forward or aft when jibing the spinnaker? *Forward.*
9. If you are on port tack and the next set will be on starboard, should you take the spinnaker down to windward or to leeward? *Windward.*
10. What is "projected area"? *The amount of sail facing the wind.*

CHAPTER 5

1. What is "VMG"? *Velocity made good.*
2. Which is easier to use when working with polar diagrams, true wind angle or apparent wind angle? *Apparent.*
3. What is an "AWI"? *Apparent wind indicator.*

CHAPTER 6

1. Which comes first, the warning signal or the preparatory signal? *Warning.*
2. Which represents the true starting sequence time, the gun or the shape? *Shape.*
3. What is a Vanderbilt start? *A timed start.*
4. What is an "oscillating shift"? *One that shifts back and forth.*
5. How do you determine the "favored" end of the starting line? *Determine the upwind end.*
6. What does pointing the boat at the windward mark tell you? *The long tack and which jibe if windward/leeward course.*
7. What is a "current stick"? *A weighted stick dropped next to a fixed buoy to determine velocity and direction of the current.*
8. What is a "dip start"? *An approach from the course side of the line, crossing the line totally before the start.*
9. Why would you do a "delayed start"? *To be able to tack to port without being pinned down by a windward starboard tack boat.*

10. What benefits are there in a port tack start? *If you cross all the boats at starboard tack, you are leading the fleet.*

CHAPTER 7

1. What is a "safe leeward position"? *Ahead and to leeward of a windward boat.*
2. What is backwind? *Turbulent air off the sails of a lead boat.*
3. Name one way of breaking cover. *Tack away when covering boat is preoccupied.*
4. What is a "loose" cover? *To windward but not hurting the leeward boat.*
5. What are "lines of equal position"? *Lines perpendicular to the wind direction.*
6. Why should you avoid laylines? *Any shift, whether a header or a lift, hurts your position.*
7. Should you round a leeward mark very closely? *Only at the end of a wide turn.*
8. When is a boat tacking? *From head-to-wind to close-hauled on the other tack.*
9. When can a leeward boat luff after starting? *When a boat is passing to windward.*
10. I'm close-hauled on port tack approaching a windward mark. Can I demand buoy room from a starboard tack boat? *No.*
11. How does the "zone" affect buoy room rights? *Once inside the zone, an inside boat must be given room to round it.*

CHAPTER 8

1. What is the most important factor in steering that makes one helmsman better than another? *Concentration.*
2. Where should crew weight be in drifting conditions? *To leeward.*
3. Does current run faster in deeper or shallower water? *Deeper.*
4. How can you judge what effect the current is having on your boat? *By use of a range.*
5. What is "lee-bow" current? *Current that is flowing toward the leeward side of your bow.*

CHAPTER 9

1. If a shroud breaks, what is the first thing to do? *Change tacks.*

2. To steer without a rudder, how do you head off? *Ease the mainsail.*

3. What can happen if you quickly turn a boat that's full of water? *The water keeps moving forward and the boat capsizes.*

4. What indicates an intense squall? *A low pink tinge.*

5. What do three vertical lights on a powerboat indicate to you? *A tow 200 meters behind.*

6. Which sail is doused first in a squall? *The largest one.*

7. What is a "warp"? *A line towed astern to slow the boat.*

8. What is "kedging"? *Taking an anchor out and pulling the boat off of aground.*

9. What is the Morse Code distress signal? ●●●‒‒‒●●●

10. What is the origin of the word "Mayday"? *French* m'aider *meaning "help me."*

Glossary

abeam at right angles to the boat

accidental jibe an unexpected boom swing. *See also* jibe.

aft at, near, or toward the stern

angle of attack angle of boat's centerline to water flow

angle of incidence angle of sails to the apparent wind

apparent wind the vector wind caused by the true wind in combination with the boat's forward motion; the wind you feel

astern behind the boat

athwartship across the boat

back (a sail) to push a sail to windward (against the wind)

backing wind wind direction shifting counterclockwise, such as W to SW

backstay wire from upper part of mast aft to deck; a component of standing rigging

backwind wind off the jib hitting the lee side of the main

balance to neutralize forces so boat sails on a straight course with little helm

batten a slat inserted in the leech of a sail

batten pocket pocket for battens in the leech of a sail

beam the widest part of the boat

beam reach sailing with the wind abeam

bearing the angle to an object

beat a series of tacks

Bernoulli's Principle as velocity of air increases air pressure decreases. Air picks up speed as it flows behind the jib and mainsail. The reduction in air pressure creates lift, causing the sails to pull the boat forward.

blanketed deprived of wind in the sails by another boat or large object to windward

boom horizontal spar that supports foot of sail

boom vang device to keep the boom from lifting

bow forward end of the boat

bowline a common knot used by sailors to form a loop (pronounced bolin)

bow wave the initial wave created by the bow breaking the water

broad reach sailing between a beam reach and a run; sailing with the wind on the quarter

by the lee wind on same side of the boat as boom when running

camber belly of a sail

capsize to overturn a boat

center of buoyancy (CB) The point around which the forces pushing upward to keep a boat afloat are concentrated. The CB will be located somewhere on the fore-and-aft centerline of a well-trimmed boat at rest, but as the boat heels and its wetted surface changes, the CB moves to leeward, thus resisting further heeling. *See also* center of gravity.

center of effort (CE) The theoretical point in a boat's sail plan at which the wind's pressure is focused. The fore-and-aft relationship between the CE and the center of lateral resistance (CLR) determines a boat's helm balance. *See also* center of lateral resistance.

center of gravity (CG) The geometric center through which all weights in a boat act vertically downward. If you could suspend a boat from its CG, it would hang perfectly level. In a keelboat the CG is located deep in the hull, giving it "ballast stability." The relationship between the CG and the center of buoyancy (CB) creates a "righting arm" that causes the boat to favor an upright position. As the boat heels and the CB moves farther leeward from the CG, the righting arm grows in strength, thus resisting further heeling.

center of lateral resistance (CLR) The imaginary vertical line through a boat's underwater profile that divides the underwater area into two equal halves, forward and aft. The CLR is like the axis of a weather vane. If you were strong enough to place your forefinger on a boat's CLR and push it sideways, it would yield without pivoting. The relationship between the CLR and the center of effort (CE) dictates the boat's tendency to either round up into the wind or fall off. Simply put, if the CE is located aft of the CLR, the boat will have weather helm—it will pivot toward the wind. If the CE is forward of the CLR, the boat will have lee helm.

chock guide on deck for docklines or anchor rode to pass through

chord straight-line distance from luff to leech on a sail

cleat device to secure a line

clew the aft corner of a sail

close-hauled sailing as close as possible to the wind

close-reach sailing between closehauled and a beam reach

come about to change tacks with the bow turning through the wind; to tack

cringle a reinforced hole sewn or pressed into a sail through which a line can be passed

cunningham device to tension the luff of a mainsail

current water flowing in a definite direction

Dacron synthetic material used in sail manufacture

daysailer small sailboat

displacement total weight of the boat

douse quickly lowering sails

downwind sailing with the wind pushing from behind

draft distance from waterline to boat's lowest part

draft (of a sail) as seen from above, the distance from the straight-line chord between a sail's luff and leech to the deepest point of the sail's curve, or camber

ease to let out, as in a sheet

fairlead a fitting through which a line passes, changing the line's direction

fall off to turn the boat away from the wind

feathering to sail so close to the wind that sails luff periodically

foot (of sail) bottom edge of a sail

footing increasing speed by falling off slightly

foredeck the deck forward of the mast or foremast

forestay any wire that runs from foredeck up to mast for setting a jib and supporting the mast

forward toward the bow

fractional rig forestay runs from bow to at least three-quarters up the mast, but not to the top

furl to fold a lowered sail and secure it

gennaker asymmetrical, lightweight reaching jib

genoa jib whose clew overlaps the mast

gooseneck swivel fitting attaching the boom to mast

gust a sudden increase in wind velocity, also called a puff

halyard wire or line that pulls the sail up

hank a fastener by which a sail is attached to a stay

harden up turn the boat toward the wind

head (of sail) the top corner of the sail

header wind shift toward the bow

headstay the foremost stay from bow to top of mast

headway/steerageway forward motion, enough to steer effectively

heeling when a sailboat leans to the lee

hull body of boat

hull speed boat's theoretical maximum speed

in irons/in stays head to wind and dead in the water

jib foresail carried on the jibstay

jib hanks snaps to connect jib to stay

jib lead adjustable fairlead for jibsheets, determines angle of jibsheet to the clew

jibe to change tacks downwind

jibsheet line tied to clew of jib or genoa that adjusts sail in and out

jibstay wire from bow to mast (but not to masthead)

jiffy reef reef in the mainsail that is tied rather than rolled

keel vertical fin under boat with weight for stability

knockdown boat is blown over such that both mast and keel lie at waterline

leech the trailing edge of a sail

leech cord small line running up inside leech to reduce flutter

lee helm bow turns to leeward when tiller is released

leeward in the direction opposite from which the wind is blowing (pronounced looward)

leeway side-slipping to leeward

length at waterline (LWL) distance between points where bow and stern touch the water at rest

length overall (LOA) distance from the tip of bow to end of stern

lift wind shift toward the stern

lower shrouds shrouds that lead from base of spreaders to deck

luff spill wind out of a sail

luff (of a sail) the leading edge of the sail

lull sudden reduction in wind velocity

main short for mainsail

main halyard line that raises and lowers the mainsail

Glossary

mainsail sail hoisted along after edge of mainmast (pronounced mainsl)

mast vertical spar supporting sails

mast step plate that holds bottom of mast in place

masthead top of mast

masthead fly device at top of mast to indicate wind direction

masthead rig jibstay runs from top of mast to bow of boat

messenger light line used to feed heavier line or blocks to areas not easily reached

neutral helm no tug on the tiller; no weather or lee helm

no-go zone area between close-hauled and directly into wind where boat cannot sail and is dead in the water, in irons

outhaul line attached to clew of sail on a boom that adjusts foot tension

overpowered excessive heeling in comparison to forward drive

pinch to sail too close to the wind to maintain speed

planing exceeding theoretical hull speed by skimming the water

play to adjust trim in and out constantly

point to sail close to the wind

points of sail close-hauled, reaching, and running; describe relationship between wind direction and boat's heading

port side the boat's left side

port tack sailing with the main boom on starboard side

preventer a line tied to a boom to prevent an accidental jibe

puff a gust of wind, *see* gust

reach sailing with the wind across the boat

reef to shorten or reduce size of sail

rigging all the wire and rope on a boat

roach convex area of sail lying aft of a straight line from head to clew when viewed from the side

roller-furling jib headsail that rolls up vertically

rudder underwater fin turned by tiller or wheel to steer the boat

run sailing with the wind from behind the boat

running rigging all lines, tackles, etc., that adjust the sails

set describes a sail that is raised and full of wind

sheets lines attached to clew of sails to adjust trim

shooting to turn directly into the wind

shrouds wires running abeam from masthead to the deck that hold up the mast

slot effect tendency of jib to make mainsail more effective

spinnaker a light parachute-like sail for sailing downwind

spinnaker pole spar to position tack of spinnaker

spinnaker sheet line to clew of spinnaker opposite the pole

spreader struts that spread the angle shrouds make with the mast

stall inability of wind to stay attached to lee side of sail

standing rigging all the fixed rigging that holds up masts (shrouds and stays)

starboard side the boat's right side

starboard tack sailing with the main boom on port side

stays wires from the mast to the bow and stern that keep the mast from falling forward or aft

staysail small jib tacked between mast and headstay

steerageway enough speed to steer effectively

stern extreme after end of a vessel

tabling edging on the leech of a sail

tack to change tacks with the bow passing through the wind

tack (of boat) *see* port tack and starboard tack

tack (of sail) forward lower corner

telltales wool or other light strips of material placed on shrouds or sail to show wind direction or flow

tiller arm fitted to rudderpost to steer by

traveler track running athwartship to change mainsail's angle

trim (fore and aft) the attitude of the boat, bow up or bow down

trim (sail) to pull in, to adjust the set

true north direction to the geographical north pole

true wind the wind as felt when stationary

ultimate stability ability of boat to resist turning over

veering wind direction shifting clockwise, such as S to SW

warp threads that run lengthwise in sailcloth

weather helm tendency of boat to head into the wind when helm is released

winch a drum with gears and handle to assist pulling in lines under strain

windward in the direction from which the wind is blowing

wing and wing sailing downwind with jib on one side and main on opposite side

Index

Index

Index

ORDER BLANK FOR *FAST TRACK TO SAILING*
published by International Marine/McGraw-Hill

NAME _____

ADDRESS _____

Please send me _____ copies @ $19.95 each
plus $3.00 each postage and handling.

Mail to: Offshore Sailing School, Ltd.
16731 McGregor Blvd.,
Fort Myers, FL 33908
Tel.: (239) 454-1700